READING WORKSHOP 2.0

SUPPORTING READERS in the DIGITAL AGE

Frank Serafini

HEINEMANN
Portsmouth, NH

Heinemann
361 Hanover Street
Portsmouth, NH 03801–3912
www.heinemann.com

Offices and agents throughout the world

Cataloging-in-Publication Data is on file at the Library of Congress.
ISBN: 978-0-325-05754-5

Editor: Holly Kim Price
Production: Victoria Merecki
Cover and text designs: Monica Ann Crigler
Typesetter: Valerie Levy, Drawing Board Studios
Manufacturing: Steve Bernier

Printed in the United States of America on acid-free paper

19 18 17 16 15 VP 1 2 3 4 5

This book is dedicated to Lyn Searfoss and Ralph Peterson, two of my first professors in the teacher education program at Arizona State University. You started me on this journey many years ago, and I have never looked back. Thank you for seeing something in me that many others didn't.

CONTENTS

ACKNOWLEDGMENTS

I would like to thank all of the amazing people at Heinemann who have supported my work for the past fifteen years: Holly Kim Price, Sarah Fournier, Eric Chalek, Cherie Bartlett, and other members of the editorial, marketing, and production staffs shepherded this book, and all my other writings, through to completion. Michelle Flynn, Cheryl Murphy-Savage, and others in the Speakers Bureau kept me busy presenting and working through my ideas on the road. Cathy Brophy always kept me in mind when webinars were being scheduled. Thank you all for what you have done on my behalf.

I would like to thank my sister, Suzette Youngs, for starting the conversations that led to this book. Suzette, you are always there for me to bounce ideas off, and our talks always make my writing and thinking so much better.

To all of the students who have sat through my elementary and college classes over the years, thank you for teaching me how to teach and for letting me fall on my face from time to time. Your patience is greatly appreciated.

Finally, I would like to thank Lindsey Moses for letting me into her life. Lindsey, you always challenge me to be a better teacher and writer and, most importantly, to be a better human being.

INTRODUCTION: POWERING UP!

Now is the time to understand the rich history of what we have thought books have done for us and what we think digital texts might do differently.

—Andrew Piper, 2012

I have been reading and writing about workshop approaches to literacy instruction for the past twenty-five years. One might think that I'd have run out of things to say about these instructional approaches and classroom frameworks a long time ago. Alas, that is not to be. It seems there is more to say about the changes that have taken place in literacy education, in particular, the changes in technology and digital resources that have affected the ways we teach children to read and write and how we organize classrooms to support this endeavor. Like Andrew Piper (2012) suggests in the opening epigraph, it is time to contemplate the rich history of printed books and the ways we teach children to read them. It is also time to consider the role of digital texts and how web-based resources might support the work we do in a reading workshop 2.0 environment.

Drawing on my previous work focusing on the reading workshop (Serafini 2001; Serafini and Youngs 2006), lessons in comprehension (Serafini 2004), and reading assessment (Serafini 2010a), this book will provide teachers and literacy educators with an expanded vision for the reading workshop. This vision includes new web-based and digital resources to support accessing and navigating children's literature and multimodal texts, new technologies for sharing and analyzing complex texts, and new instructional approaches for supporting readers on their journey to becoming more engaged, literate human beings in the twenty-first century.

Into my previous discussions and writing about reading workshop approaches I am now inserting the concept of reading workshop 2.0 (two-point-oh). For many teachers, the attachment of *2.0* to the term *reading workshop* may seem like an unwelcome addition to an already overcrowded curriculum, just one more thing to worry about covering during the upcoming school year. That is not my intention here. The last thing I want to do is give teachers more components to add to their reading workshop or one more thing to add to their curriculum. The instructional approaches offered throughout this book are not intended to add any additional burdens to teachers' workload or suggest new components for the reading workshop. Instead, I believe the various web-based and digital resources presented in this book will help teachers do the same important things they have been doing in the reading workshop for years, only using new resources and technologies to help children become sophisticated readers in more effective, efficient, and engaging ways.

Technology and Reading

The term *technology* can be misleading. When people say the word *technology*, they often mean the newest gizmo, software application, or digital resource that is being bandied about by friends in and out of education. However, it is important to remember that the pen and pencil were also important technological advances at one time in our history. So was the *codex*, or what we commonly refer to now as a printed book. Writing a book like *Reading Workshop 2.0* requires attending to all forms of technology, print- and digital-based, not just the newest web-based resource or trendy app to hit the Internet.

A reading workshop 2.0 framework must also take into account what Lankshear and Knobel (2006) refer to as the *new ethos stuff*, in addition to addressing the *new technical stuff*. By new ethos stuff, they are suggesting that along with the changes in the technologies teachers and readers are exposed to in and out of school, the ways in which these new technologies affect the way we interact with information, people, and ideas have also changed. The profiles people construct on various social media platforms, the relationships that develop among participants in chatrooms and discussion boards, and the conventions and expectations for communicating with colleagues through email have changed as much as the web-based platforms used to house these interactions. As readers draw on new technologies (new technical stuff), they are no longer viewed simply as consumers of information; rather, they are considered producers and critics of information as well (new ethos stuff). You will read more about the development of web-based and digital resources and the new ethos associated with it in the opening chapters.

Creating New Spaces

In 2001 when I wrote my first book for Heinemann, *The Reading Workshop: Creating Space for Readers*, the concept of *space* in the subtitle was conceptualized primarily in terms of physical space—the physical organization, layout, and resources necessary for enacting a reading workshop framework within the four walls of the classroom. With the expansion and increased availability of web-based and digital resources since I wrote that book, the space being conceptualized in this new book has both physical and virtual dimensions. Creating space for readers and reading in a reading workshop 2.0 environment means addressing the role of web-based and digital resources, in addition to the print-based texts and resources traditionally found in brick-and-mortar classroom settings. The resources and instructional approaches suggested for supporting a reading workshop 2.0 framework are a way of expanding and reconceptualizing the traditional, physical spaces associated with literacy instruction in my early writing on the reading workshop.

Today children's and young adult novels, textbooks, picture books, and informational texts are provided in both print-based and digital formats; book reviews are posted online for anyone in the world to read; and readers continue to access information through web-based and digital technologies. The physical and virtual spaces we develop to support and foster our children's literate abilities must take advantage of these new resources and their instructional possibilities. The resources teachers need for supporting children's development into sophisticated readers in the digital age extend well beyond the walls of the traditional classroom.

Readers and Reading in the Digital Age

What it takes to become a successful reader grows more complex with every generation. Web-based and digital resources require different skills and reading strategies than the literacy skills and strategies needed by our parents. Because of these changes, the traditional reading skills used to decode print-based texts should be viewed as *necessary, but insufficient* given the complexity of contemporary texts, web-based and digital resources, and social media platforms students encounter in and out of schools (Freebody and Luke 1990; Serafini 2012a). Reading has always been more than decoding; the skills and strategies necessary for success in web-based and digital environments are just becoming more obvious given the complexity of the texts and resources readers encounter now. Students will need to develop a more extensive array of literacy skills, strategies, and practices to be successful using these new texts and resources in the new millennium.

In today's digital age, readers encounter new technologies that mediate and support their transactions with a variety of print-based and digital texts. They have access to texts that include visual images, background music, and hyperlinks, in addition to written language. These complex, *multimodal texts* convey information and communicate through many different resources or modes.

Simply put, a *multimodal text* is one that uses more than one *mode* or system of meaning for representing and communicating ideas and information (see Kress 2010; Serafini 2014). A mode is a resource—photography, sculpture, poetry, music, mathematics, paintings, and typography are some examples—used to convey ideas and information. A multimodal text is simply a text that contains more than one mode, like a picture book or website. Therefore, multimodal texts require readers to develop skills and strategies beyond the traditional skills of decoding, visualizing, predicting, and summarizing. Readers in the digital age need strategies for attending to resources beyond written language—such as visual images, design elements, and typography—to make sense of these complex texts.

Today most readers have some access to the Internet in school or at home. This access provides readers with many new web-based and digital resources, including social media platforms, presentation tools, reference materials, and informational warehouses unknown to previous generations. For example, many famous museums now provide images of their works of art, history, and science that were once only available by visiting their physical locations. With a computer linked to the Internet, readers can take virtual tours of the Metropolitan Museum of Art in New York City, the Smithsonian Institute in Washington, D.C., and the Art Institute of Chicago in a single day without leaving their classrooms. Of course, seeing these works of art, history, and science on a computer screen isn't the same as seeing them in person, but access to these collections is now possible for more people than ever, at home or in class, on their own time and on a limited budget.

In the digital age, *digital bookshelves* have begun to replace the stacks of printed texts that have for years lined the walls of homes, schools, universities, and local libraries. Today readers can carry hundreds of books and documents on their electronic tablets and share their ideas instantaneously with readers from around the world via their smartphones. The possibility of sharing ideas with readers of such diverse backgrounds changes how we conceive of and organize literature study groups in new and exciting ways. Knowing what a reader from Australia thinks about a headline in a Russian newspaper or how a pen pal from Scotland reacts to an excerpt from a classic Victorian novel enables readers in our classrooms to expand their own perspectives on current events and literature beyond the confines of their immediate circle of friends.

The digital age has also provided new technologies for archiving discussions and instructional episodes in ways not available in the analog era. Classroom-based websites, audio recordings of discussions, video clips of lessons, electronic portfolios of students' work documenting their literacy development, and digital histories of school and classroom events are now easily documented and archived for instant retrieval.

The technologies available for accessing a wide variety of texts, sharing ideas about what has been read, conducting discussions across time and space, and analyzing complex, multimodal resources are expanding so fast it is difficult to keep up. What our children read, how they access these texts, and the platforms available for responding to what they read present a variety of challenges for today's teachers. It is also important to remember that our focus must remain on the act of reading itself (Ulin 2010)—whether it's flipping through the pages of a hardcover book or scrolling down the screen of an eReader. We cannot throw the proverbial baby out with the bath water as we consider the possibilities presented by new technologies and how they can support and challenge readers in the digital age. As educators, I believe we are just beginning to understand the educational potential for many of these web-based and digital resources and technologies.

Children in the Digital Age

According to a recent *New York Times* survey, millenials (people born approximately between 1985 and 2000) access online resources about fifteen hours a day, on average. Texting, posting on social media sites, emailing, pinning photos on the web, and sharing information with one's friends take up a larger and larger part of our children's lives. We need to find ways to ensure that our children continue to become critical, successful users of these technologies, operating in safe environments throughout our schools and at home.

Children are just as social today as they were many years ago. Interacting with friends is still more important to most kids than learning algebra—the biggest difference today is simply the tools children use to connect with their friends. As opportunities for meeting up with peers in physical spaces continue to decrease and become less attractive to parents, like malls and street corners, children turn to social media and their smartphones to stay connected with their friends. Technologies may come and go quickly, but the core activities of sharing ideas, socializing, chatting with one's friends, engaging in self-expression, and sharing information remain as important as ever (Boyd 2014). How children do these things and how teachers can take advantage of students' experiences and skills with new technologies remain important considerations as we move forward as literacy educators.

How This Book Is Organized

This book is designed to provide the necessary web-based and digital resources to help teachers support the development of sophisticated readers in these changing times and to organize their reading workshops so that they can take advantage of the latest technologies available for literacy instruction. The three chapters in Part I offer a foundation for the reading workshop and set forth the theoretical principles, pedagogical strands, and instructional components upon which reading workshop 2.0 is built. Chapter 1 presents ten theoretical principles about teaching reading that are crucial for operating from a constructivist, child-centered reading workshop perspective. These principles represent my long-held beliefs about literacy instruction and provide a theoretical foundation for the reading workshop 2.0 framework. In Chapter 2, I revisit the pedagogical strands and instructional components of the reading workshop and discuss all of the new ideas that have been part of my research on teaching reading since I last wrote about the reading workshop (Serafini and Youngs 2006). In Chapter 3, I discuss some of the shifts that support moving from a reading workshop 1.0 to a reading workshop 2.0 approach to reading and literacy education.

Part II of the book presents four reading processes that are essential for reading in the digital age. The four processes are (1) accessing and navigating,

(2) archiving and sharing, (3) commenting and discussing, and (4) interpreting and analyzing. These four processes focus on different aspects of what readers do with print-based and digital texts in the reading workshop 2.0 framework. Chapter 4, on accessing and navigating, focuses on the various ways in which readers access, navigate, and interact with print, web-based, and digital texts. Web-based texts, eReaders, online aggregators, interactive storybooks, and audio books will all be discussed in this chapter. Chapter 5, on archiving and sharing, presents some of the new technologies readers use for archiving their reading lives and sharing what they read with other readers. Chapter 6 covers commenting on and discussing digital texts. Here I offer the reader numerous strategies and resources for expanding how readers share what they think about what they have read with other readers. Examples of technologies for highlighting texts, marking up or coding digital texts, participating in real-time discussions, and using social media platforms like Goodreads.com will be shared. Chapter 7, the closing chapter of Part II, focuses on interpreting and analyzing digital texts, particularly the strategies and resources available for analyzing multimodal and digital texts. The resources provided in each chapter support readers as they transact with texts in more engaging ways, developing new analytical tools, perspectives, and approaches for interpreting and critiquing multimodal texts.

A Few Words of Caution

Some years ago, as a newly minted assistant professor at the University of Nevada, Las Vegas, I attended a workshop with a colleague. The workshop focused on the newest technologies for teaching physics. Now, to be honest, I have very little background knowledge in physics and I attended this workshop more as a social event than as a professional development opportunity. However, what became immediately clear to me was that the focus was on physics, not the technologies used to support teaching physics. The presenter was excellent and used a vast array of technologies I had never seen before, but the focus remained on learning physics. The technology was simply a tool used in service of learning about kinetic energy, acceleration, and friction. I left there convinced that the role of technology in literacy education should be exactly the same: The focus should not be on the newest technology, platform, or enhanced website for sharing ideas about books; rather, it should be on reading, reacting to what has been read, and sharing interpretations with other readers. The newest resources and technologies should be seen as simply tools to help our students make sense of the texts they encounter in deeper, more effective and efficient ways.

New technologies can be an enticing proposition. Fancy gizmos are often touted as the cure for everything from illiteracy to finding a soul mate. In the digital age we have to be wary of the vaudeville barkers auctioning off the latest *techno-bling* as the solution to all the challenges facing education. We as teachers cannot lose sight of the educational possibilities of these new technologies in our excitement over the technology itself. If a new object doesn't help children develop as sophisticated readers, it doesn't matter how shiny it is.

As you are aware, web-based technologies come and go. Teachers can quickly become overwhelmed trying to keep up with the millions of resources available and the new ones arriving online every day. Teachers have to be careful to not waste time chasing after the newest application and, in doing so, forget about all the old technologies—picture books, novels, libraries, and so forth—that have supported the development of readers and have been vital components of the reading workshop for years. The word processor, highlighters, and colored sticky notes have served us well over the years and will continue to do so. We must find ways to build upon the available educational resources that have already been proven effective rather than throw out all the old ideas that worked to find space for the new ones.

To address the rapid advances in technology offerings, throughout this book I have tried to list only those software applications and web-based resources that have been used extensively and for a sustained period of time. I have provided a minimum of three different examples of the web-based or digital resources I recommend. Now, of course, all three resources on my lists may become obsolete before I even finish writing this book, which demonstrates just how fast things are progressing. To address this challenge, I have created a web-based resource that I will continue to update with the newest, most effective resources for supporting teachers as they implement a reading workshop 2.0 approach. Please visit www.frankserafini.com/rw20.html to see what changes may have occurred since the publication of this book.

It seems that books published years ago about teaching reading had a longer shelf life than the professional books being published today. In the past, changes in technology didn't alter the basic processes of reading the way that digital technologies have changed how readers access and navigate texts today. Given the technological changes of the past twenty years, professional development resources like this book have to find new ways to address this rapidly changing environment. In the near future, web-based resources may replace print-based texts. But, for now, I feel the best professional development materials are those that offer both print-based and web-based resources that can be easily accessed and updated regularly.

I recommend reading this book with your digital reading device, tablet, smartphone, and computer close at hand. As I describe an online resource, open it on one of these devices, and play around with the various features. I have tried to describe these resources in the greatest detail possible, but by opening an app or going to a particular website yourself, your experience will be greatly enhanced.

Because of the rapidly changing nature of the resources we use to help classroom teachers, this book will actually never be finished; it will evolve as my understandings evolve. The resources I share with teachers through my website will continue to expand as my own understandings expand. Like our teaching, this book will continually evolve to support the never-ending process of developing oneself as an effective teacher.

Some Additional Thoughts

In the closing chapter of my first book, *The Reading Workshop: Creating Space for Readers*, I wrote:

> *Change is scary for many teachers, and we want things to come together in our classrooms before the end of the first week of school. However, this is rarely the case. Unsettling contradictions force us to rethink our perceptions and look closely at the experiences we provide our students. We need to be able to tolerate a degree of uncertainty if we are going to become reflective practitioners, capable of learning from our classroom experiences. (2001, 136)*

Fifteen years later, my original concerns are only amplified by the rapid changes in technology that create a more wide-ranging sense of uncertainty regarding what we teach, how we teach, and how we support our students in our reading workshops. This sense of uncertainty only adds to teachers' frustrations and concerns. What it means to be a successful reader changes quickly in the digital age. As teachers, we have to remain tolerant of the level of uncertainty associated with these rapid changes in technology and how these changes affect our children in and out of school. Only by attending to our children's needs and interests, and by becoming more highly literate beings ourselves, will we be able to provide the support and instructional experiences to help our students become sophisticated, literate human beings.

PART

I

FOUNDATIONS
OF READING
WORKSHOP 2.0

CHAPTER
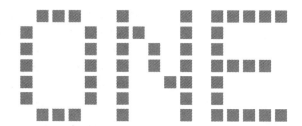

Ten Theoretical Principles About Teaching Reading

The primary goal of the reading workshop is to change the ways readers and teachers think and talk about texts from the ways readers and teachers have traditionally thought and talked about texts in classrooms.

—Frank Serafini, 2006

I am sure it is unusual for a chapter to begin with an epigraph of one's own, but this statement, which I have used as an opening slide for every professional development workshop for the past ten years, fully encapsulates my fundamental beliefs about teaching reading. I believe that the focus of the reading workshop should remain on changing the ways teachers and children talk and think about texts from the ways we have done so in schools for years. The reading workshop should not focus on teaching readers to recall literal details or identify some main idea hiding in the text. Rather, the reading workshop should be about teaching children to select, navigate, comprehend, discuss, and analyze a wide range of print and digitally based texts.

The reading workshop is not about procedures, although consistent procedures help teachers and readers organize their time in school and make sense of the experiences provided. It is not specifically about developing lesson plans, although lesson plans are an important part of the reading workshop framework. At its core, the reading workshop is about finding ways to support readers as they try to make sense of the world around them, in particular the variety of complex texts they encounter in their daily lives.

As classroom teachers, it is all too easy to get caught up in the day-to-day procedures that make up the reading workshop—forms to fill out, tables to arrange, books to shelve, lessons to plan, notebooks to respond to. These things often keep us from focusing on the real purposes for doing what we are doing. Teachers support readers by inviting children into the world of reading, creating effective learning experiences, encouraging students to think about and question what they are reading, and responding effectively to students' efforts. I don't want the minutiae of the day-to-day procedures to keep us from our primary goal of supporting readers as they make sense of what they read.

In our book *Around the Reading Workshop in 180 Days* (Serafini and Youngs 2006), we wrote the following:

> *Everything we do in the reading workshop must be done in service of making meaning. Whether we are discussing literature, investigating the relationship between written symbols and oral language, helping readers choose an appropriate book to read independently, or working on understanding the nature of the alphabet, the practices and procedures I am enacting in my reading workshop serve the primary goal of supporting readers' construction of meaning in transactions with texts. (2)*

In order to maintain the focus of the reading workshop on *changing the way we think and talk about texts,* we need to keep in mind a few things. First, we need to envision reading as an authentic, purposeful, complex process of transacting with texts. Reading real books, for real reasons, and sharing ideas with real people ensures that we keep meaning at the forefront of the reading process. Second, our teaching needs to be done "in the foam"—in the messy process of actually reading and trying to make sense of the texts in front of us.

Figure 1.1 Reading Guide for the Ten Theoretical Principles

Ask yourself the following questions as you read through the ten theoretical principles about teaching reading:

1. What does this theoretical principle mean for my current approaches to teaching reading? What things am I doing right now in my classroom that I might want to change?

2. What resources would I need to move toward the reading workshop described in these theoretical principles?

3. What challenges might arise as I work to change my instructional practices based on these theoretical principles?

4. What areas of study might I need to explore further to develop my skills as a reading teacher?

Our teaching of reading cannot begin on worksheets to hopefully be transferred back to real texts at a later time. Finally, breaking down reading into little parts only to put it back together later on will not serve our readers well in the digital age. We must keep in mind that meaning is constructed by experiencing and transacting with authentic texts in relevant and purposeful contexts.

In this chapter, I offer a list of theoretical principles about teaching reading, ten things to consider as we work together to build the pedagogical foundation for our reading workshop 2.0 framework. These principles are purposely broad-based ideas that have considerable range, flexibility, depth, and applicability. These theoretical principles are also based on an extensive array of evidence from the research of other educators and from my own classroom observations and studies.

My Ten Theoretical Principles

Principle 1. *Realize that the strategies and skills students need to comprehend the complex texts they encounter nowadays have expanded beyond the strategies for reading written text alone.*

The days of the printed novel containing no images seem numbered. Leather-bound novels, dense with print, have evolved into multimodal ensembles that blend visual images and design elements with written language to communicate and render narratives and offer information. The Diary of a Wimpy Kid series by Jeff Kinney, Sherman Alexie's *Absolutely True Story of a Part-Time Indian*, and Neil Gaiman's *The Graveyard Book* feature visual images and design elements, in addition to the written narrative. *Skeleton Creek* by Patrick Carman even requires readers to go online to watch video segments and other digital resources to continue with the story introduced in the printed novel. Informational picture books are now linked up with websites to provide information through sound effects, photography, graphs, maps, and other modes in addition to the information found in the text.

Picture books, a long-time staple of the elementary classroom, have always required reading strategies that extend beyond those for written text alone. Design elements—typography, borders, layout, end pages, and visual images such as illustrations, graphs, diagrams, and maps—all require an expanded set of literacy skills in addition to those required to access and interpret written language. When we add the interactive nature of picture books experienced on CD, digital reading devices, or websites, the strategies needed to make sense of these texts expand exponentially. As the texts readers encounter change and evolve, the strategies and knowledge base readers will need to continue to make sense of these complex, multimodal texts will need to expand and evolve as well (Serafini 2014).

What does this mean for my teaching practices?

In today's classrooms, teachers will need to develop an understanding of how to make sense of visual images and design elements in addition to teaching skills for decoding written language. Discussions will need to go beyond literal recall and simple questions to consider the meaning potential of these multimodal texts. Teaching comprehension strategies in the context of reading multimodal texts is vital for student success. We need to build upon the reading strategies students have already demonstrated—for example, monitoring for comprehension, summarizing, and asking questions—by extending these strategies to comprehend the visual images and design elements of multimodal texts.

Principle 2. *Decrease the amount of time spent standing in front of the whole class delivering lessons that work only for a few readers, and instead spend more time in small groups working at readers' points of need.*

We need to decrease the amount of *full frontal assault teaching* we do and become more *reader-centric* in our lesson plans and instructional approaches. It would be lovely if all our students needed the exact same lesson on the exact same day, but it is hard to imagine this being the case. Even with the most extensive assessment data available it is hard to imagine that we can know exactly what everyone in our class needs at a given moment. Unfortunately, what usually happens in whole-group instruction is that teachers meet the needs of some readers, bore a few others, and confuse the rest.

Our whole-group lessons should serve as invitations to and demonstrations of trying new strategies, resources, and reading practices that allow all readers a point of entry into what is being taught. Differentiation is best accomplished when we work in small groups, pairs, or one-on-one with readers to reinforce those skills and strategies we have introduced in whole-group lessons. Small-group instruction designed to help readers at their points of need is a key component of the reading workshop 2.0 framework.

What does this mean for my teaching practices?

For many teachers, the question becomes, "What do I do with the rest of the class while I am doing small-group instruction?" In order to leave the front of the classroom behind, teachers have to set procedures and scaffolds in place that support students' independence. For me, the time spent in the first months of the school year setting up procedures and expectations for students to be more self-sufficient is worth its weight in gold.

In my reading workshop framework, I try to follow a 60–40 ratio, meaning that during more than half (60 percent) of my scheduled workshop time readers should be reading and exploring texts independently, in pairs, or in small groups rather than listening to me deliver a lesson or demonstrate a strategy in front of the room. We have to provide enough time each day for readers to really engage with a variety of texts, and we can't provide this time if they are always sitting around watching us conduct whole-class lessons. The 40 percent of the workshop time should be when students are involved in demonstrations and learning experiences that help them transact with texts. Sustained silent reading, reading strategy instruction in small groups, self-selected reading, and time to explore narrative and informational texts are essential components of the reading workshop. As teachers, we need to find ways to work beside readers as well as conduct lessons in front of them.

Principle 3. *Demonstrate how to approach, navigate, and closely analyze a wide variety of texts.*

As sophisticated and proficient readers, we stand in front of our students reading aloud fluently, talking about what books mean, and sharing our analyses of complex texts. But to many of the readers in our classrooms, how we do this is a mystery. For many children, reading remains an invisible process until we as teachers demonstrate through *think-alouds* what we are doing. We have to learn how to unpack what we do as readers by making our thinking and reading *visible* so that our readers can begin to understand the strategies and literary practices involved in being a sophisticated reader.

One of the most important things we do as literacy educators is provide effective demonstrations for our students of what successful readers do. In addition, these demonstrations help to maintain our primary focus on talking and thinking about texts. Although I do not want teachers standing in front of students all day long, I do want them to spend part of the workshop time introducing the strategies and processes their students will need to develop into more sophisticated readers.

In current educational settings, close reading has become an important concept. Close reading is an intentional and analytical type of reading that teachers are being asked to demonstrate and instill in our readers in our classrooms. In order to help readers read closely, we have to be able to demonstrate what close reading looks and sounds like. We have to be able to think aloud in front of our students to create a space for discussing this particular type of reading and analysis so that our readers can begin to assimilate these literary practices.

What does this mean for my teaching practices?

Our demonstrations should be conducted with a wide variety of texts—narrative and expository texts, novels and picture books, poetry and textbooks—and should call students' attention to the textual, hypertextual, visual, and design elements of what is being read. As teachers, we have to be able to stand in front of our students and demonstrate the slow, deliberate, analytical processes of making sense of short sections of text to help readers learn to do this type of reading on their own. By demonstrating close readings of texts and images to our students, supporting them as they attempt to emulate what we have demonstrated, and providing time for our readers to apply these skills and strategies, we are helping them become more analytical and thoughtful readers themselves.

Principle 4. *Reduce the dominance of the fictional novel in the reading curriculum to allow room for the other types of texts that readers in contemporary society enjoy.*

I begin by suggesting that my reading life has changed drastically in the last ten years. And, I believe, so have the reading lives of the many of the children I work with in both elementary and college settings. Some of the biggest changes that have taken place revolve around what I read, how I access what I read, and how I respond to my readings. Where I once sat by myself in a comfortable chair reading fictional novels, I now have my iPad next to me so I can share my thoughts about what I have read online, send book suggestions via email or text messages to my friends, and have instant access to a connected set of texts that often include visual images, sound effects, or video segments.

In my current situation as a professor of children's and young adult literature, my reading life is rarely if ever dominated by the fictional novel. I read professional books and articles, picture books, online essays and blogs, book reviews, magazines and newspapers in print and digital formats, social media posts, and the endless "tweets" from my Twitter feed. Of course, I do continue to read and enjoy fictional novels for adults, children, and young adults as part of my personal and professional life, but my reading life is more diverse now than ever.

The dominance of the print-based, fictional novel in our society is waning and so should its stranglehold on reading instructional approaches. As children move up in grade levels, they are often required to read more fictional novels each and every year. As students graduate from elementary school, picture books are often replaced with novels and textbooks. A quick look at the Exemplar Texts offered in Appendix B of the Common Core Standards website (www.corestandards.org) will confirm this trend. When so many of the texts readers engage with outside of school feature multimodal and digital components, why does the list of required readings in schools still look like a suggested reading list from the 1970s?

What does this mean for my teaching practices?

Our classroom libraries and read-aloud sessions must feature the same wide variety of texts we find in the world outside of schools. The goal is to help readers become successful with more types of texts than simply the school-based genres that have dominated educational settings for years. Readers need to be allowed to read graphic novels, comic books, video catalogues and manuals, magazines, newspapers, and other authentic reading materials in addition to those genres traditionally endorsed in school settings. Author studies focusing on picture book illustrators, units of study focusing on various types of magazines, reading poetry, accessing informational texts, and navigating video and image-based essays all need to be included in greater proportions in our reading workshop. As we begin to investigate these new genres, formats, and text features, we might find that reading three to five novels a year in the elementary grades is enough.

Principle 5. *Foster a sense of independence in one's readers.*

Real-life readers do not wait for someone to tell them what to read next, nor do they wonder what to do when they are done reading. These life-long readers seek out new books, share the ones they have read with their friends, and work to make sense of what they are reading. In the reading workshop, we are not trying to teach children to read to get better at playing school or even to get better at reading itself, although these are wonderful side effects. Our goals as reading teachers are grander than that. We are teaching children to read to help them understand the world around them and their place in it, as well as the lives and experiences of others. Getting better at reading is simply a by-product of spending time reading, talking, and learning from one another. Our goal is to help children become more sophisticated, independent readers who choose to read based on their own needs, interests, and experiences.

We take away our readers' sense of independence when we don't allow them to choose what they can read, limit their access to only certain texts, and always decide where and when they are allowed to read. Readers with a sense of independence choose what they read. They choose where and when they read and for what purposes. They share books with other readers and expect friends to make recommendations for their own reading selections. We have to establish classroom rituals, procedures, and expectations that support rather than detract from developing our students' sense of independence as readers.

What does this mean for my teaching practices?

We have to help readers learn techniques for finding and selecting texts that will interest them and serve their purposes so that they can explore the wide range of reading material available. We need to provide access to a wide variety of texts to allow readers real choices. We have to help readers respond to texts and share their ideas through the many vehicles we will provide throughout the reading workshop. And sometimes we have to step back and let students act and decide for themselves, whether or not we think they are right. Only through practice and trial and error will our students develop as independent readers.

Principle 6. *Organize the reading workshop in response to the needs, skills, and interests of the readers in one's classrooms.*

In order to organize our reading workshops around the needs, skills, and interests of our readers, we need to begin by getting to know them as people and as readers. In my book *Classroom Reading Assessments: More Efficient Ways to View and Evaluate Your Readers* (Serafini 2010a), I offered a framework for assessing children's reading abilities and getting to know them as readers. The biggest challenge is how to use this information to effectively organize the learning experiences we provide in our reading workshop.

In order to understand children as readers, we need to draw upon a variety of assessment instruments. Through the use of reader interviews, oral reading analyses, reading conferences, think-aloud protocols, and reader response notebooks we come to know our students as readers. Each year the group of students we work with is different. One year a group will love a particular book, and in other years readers may not enjoy that book at all. We have to remain sensitive to these changes so that we can be responsive to the needs and interests of the children that arrive on our doorsteps each fall.

What does this mean for my teaching practices?

This theoretical principle means we will be spending the first few weeks and months of school getting to know our students as readers through the myriad of assessments we have available to us. We need to conduct interest inventories, reader interviews, running records or miscue analyses, think-aloud protocols, and reading response activities to get to know our students' strengths and limitations. The assessments we conduct should provide us with a wide range of information to help us get a more extensive understanding of our readers' needs and skills. We cannot create a reader-centric reading workshop until we get to know the readers in our classes.

Principle 7. *Read aloud every day from a variety of texts and for a variety of purposes.*

In *Reading Aloud and Beyond: Fostering the Intellectual Life with Older Readers* (Serafini and Giorgis 2003), we offered thirteen scientifically based reasons for reading aloud with readers of every age. These reasons included: Reading aloud demonstrates fluent reading; it provides access to texts readers may not be able to read independently; it builds a stronger classroom community; and it creates a space for thinking and discussions.

Readers, especially those who state they do not like to read, often do not know about the wide variety of texts available in the world of literature. It is up to us as classroom teachers and teacher educators to help children discover new literary treasures every day. The easiest way to do this is by reading aloud to our students. We want readers to make connections to a variety of authors, illustrators, and story characters; to become invested in the books they read; and to acquire strong appetites for literature and reading. Reading aloud is one of the most effective and efficient ways of doing these things.

Reading aloud sets the foundation for many of the essential components of the reading workshop. As teachers, we read aloud to foster intellectual discussions, demonstrate proficient reader strategies, increase students' vocabularies, and introduce readers to new genres, authors, illustrators, and content areas. All of this allows readers to develop their identities as fellow readers and opens up the world of literature for them.

What does this mean for my teaching practices?

We need to rethink our idea of what reading aloud really is. More than just a fun thing to do each day, it is an important instructional practice. Yes, reading aloud is an enjoyable daily experience for both students and teachers, but it is also an important instructional component of the reading workshop framework. We give more time to those elements of our reading instruction that we find valuable, so by reconceptualizing reading aloud as a worthwhile instructional component we will want to dedicate more time to it. Read aloud each and every day to your students. Be purposeful in your selections and your reasons for doing so. Choose high-quality literature to read aloud, and allow time for readers to talk about what has been read. Every time we pick up a favorite book and share it with our students, we foster the love of reading.

Principle 8. *Learn how to facilitate sophisticated discussions about the texts being read and shared.*

In his professional development book *Tell Me: Children, Reading, and Talk* (Chambers 1996), Aidan Chambers suggests that literature discussions become spaces for *shared contemplation*. Readers need to be able to offer ideas in the spirit of communal investigation, a space where "half-baked" ideas can be offered and considered without fear of retribution. In my book *Interactive Comprehension Strategies: Fostering Meaningful Talk About Texts* (Serafini 2009), I offer numerous strategies for fostering more intellectual discussions, creating spaces for readers to share their ideas, and developing more sophisticated analytical tools for readers to use when reading and discussing fiction and expository texts.

Unfortunately, the ways teachers talk to children and the language used by teachers in classroom settings have actually changed very little in the past fifty years. How teachers talk and the types of questions they ask have been *institutionalized* through the various educational entities that prepare and support teachers. We learn to talk with children the same way we were talked to as students. We also learned how to talk with children from watching our mentor teachers, as we became teachers. To change the traditional ways of talking with children, we have to pay close attention to how we talk with them and find new ways of interacting around literature.

The talk that occurs in the reading workshop should support sophisticated thinking and intellectual complexity, not simply literal recall and recitation. We want to draw upon language that supports *mindfulness*, not passivity. We need to set explicit, clear, and obtainable expectations for our classroom discussions. Talk is essential for the intellectual and social development of all children. For some children, the talk in which they engage at school is nothing less than a lifeline. It is through talk that we create and re-create our identities, develop relationships with other people, come to understand the world, and share the experiences we have with others.

What does this mean for my teaching practices?

We need to create more effective spaces for students to share what they have read and are thinking. We can do this by asking fewer literal questions, piggybacking on what students have already offered, and increasing the percentage of student talk versus teacher talk. The questions we do ask need to extend students' thinking, helping them to reconsider their own ideas in light of new ones. We need to help readers assume responsibility for articulating their ideas in our community of readers and to listen to what other students are saying and through this be able to reconsider their own thinking.

Principle 9. *Develop a sense of wonder and teach readers how to tolerate the ambiguity inherent in many texts and experiences.*

Stories help us understand the world and our place in it. We learn to delight in the playful language of Dr. Seuss, wander through the imaginative worlds created by David Wiesner, and tremble at the horrors awaiting us in *The Hunger Games* (Collins 2008). Even more important than becoming immersed in the wonders of the stories we read, our own lives are illuminated by the experiences offered by our favorite fictional narratives. We need to approach stories as we approach our everyday experiences, with a sense of wonder and enjoyment.

Great literature doesn't tell us *how* to act, or what to think, or whom to become. Rather, great literature offers us *choices and insights* into how we might act, who we might become, and what we might think. The ambiguity inherent in great literature should be seen not as a hurdle to overcome but as an opportunity for disrupting our traditional and stereotypical ways of thinking. By tolerating the ambiguity inherent in quality literature, we postpone or suspend the closure of our thinking, providing time and space for considering new and alternative ways of thinking.

The most important thing readers should get from reading a book is the desire to read another. As teachers, we cannot allow school to squash this desire. By not allowing readers to ever choose what they read, by making them do mindless activities after they finish reading, and by giving them quizzes in the name of comprehension assessment, we drive the desire to become a reader further and further underground. The experiences readers have in our schools need to enhance their sense of wonder, tickle their imaginations, and help them learn to dwell in stories and to revel in their adventures.

What does this mean for my teaching practices?

We have to accept that we don't know what every book means and that we are often left wondering about things after we finish reading. And we have to demonstrate our fallibilities to our students. The desire to reach closure with every book often limits our students' thinking and inquiry. We have to demonstrate our tolerance for ambiguity if we want our readers to feel that it's okay not to be able to answer every question. Experiences, like the texts we read, allow for multiple interpretations and reactions. These multiple interpretations create a sense of uneasiness in our drive to get the correct answer. Reading, like life, is just more complicated than finding the hidden main idea.

Principle 10. *Explore the potential for web-based and digital tools available to support the instructional practices in the reading workshop.*

This last theoretical principle is the basic premise of this book. I want to make teachers aware of the digital and web-based resources available and the instructional possibilities for using these resources in their reading workshops. The goal is not to add to the reading workshop curriculum per se; rather, it is to support readers and reading through the use of new resources and communication technologies.

As new technologies continue to enrich and challenge our lives and experiences, we as teachers need to embrace the opportunities rather than avoid them through lack of knowledge or insecurities associated with how rapidly technology is changing. Opening up our classrooms to new and innovative ideas is important, but we must keep in mind that the primary goal is still changing the way we think and talk about texts. Change for the sake of change is not the goal. Improving the learning experiences and opportunities for our children based on whatever technologies we have available is more important than chasing new trends and the latest gadgets.

What does this mean for my teaching practices?

We have to explore the web-based and digital tools available to us and become more comfortable with these resources before we try to use them in our reading workshop. Many web-based and digital tools offer tremendous potential for our teaching practices, and we are limited only by our access to them and our imaginations. The rest of this book is dedicated to helping teachers access, understand, and incorporate the wide range of new resources for supporting readers in the reading workshop.

Some Additional Thoughts

Throughout my career as a professor of literacy education and as a writer of educational books, articles, blogs, and newsletters, I have tried to describe in great detail the instructional practices I have found effective in my own teaching or observed in other classrooms for teachers to consider as they organize their own reading workshops. I have been unwilling to prescribe an inflexible set of instructional approaches or routines that are touted as working for all children, in all settings. These are *silver-bullet programs*—lessons that never really work—and besides, I feel that it is quite arrogant of me to think I have the right to tell teachers what to do every day. It is also extremely inconsiderate of the amazing teachers I work with considering their extensive knowledge and professionalism.

Instead, I have begun my books and workshops by outlining the theoretical principles that provide the foundation for my instructional practices before offering specific lessons and ideas. I have created pedagogical strands and instructional components based on these theoretical principles that support teaching and learning in the reading workshop. What is an effective practice in one context, in the hands of a particular teacher, may not translate as an effective practice in every other context with every other teacher. Teachers need to be given some autonomy to make decisions about what they feel are effective practices for their students based on the suggestions, research, and information we provide them. Classroom teachers are uniquely positioned to make effective instructional decisions based on their knowledge of their students.

Readers learn to read by reading. In some ways, it's just that simple. No one can read a book *for* you. Yes, they can read a book *to* you, but that is different. If children don't see themselves as readers, and don't see the purposes for reading, why would they ever want to become readers? We have to establish routines and procedures in the reading workshop that provide access to interesting texts, time to read, and opportunities to share what has been read.

In addition, we have to stop asking readers to do things in the name of becoming a lifelong reader that lifelong readers would never tolerate. Asking readers to build dioramas, write book reports, fill in worksheets, or participate in round-robin reading sessions simply needs to come to an end. We just need to finally say no. In place of these worthless activities and outdated instructional approaches, we need to provide readers with demonstrations of the kinds of literate practices that lifelong readers engage in as well as instructional approaches that support the development of these practices. Doing things in the name of reading instruction that do not involve actually reading and discussing real texts seems pointless to me. It is crucial that we carefully examine those instructional practices that have no base of evidence for their effectiveness other than tradition and teacher preference.

Finally, reading should not be a competition, and books should not be seen as trophies. As suggested in *Better than Life* (Pennac 1999), readers learn to read at their own pace, which may not be necessarily anybody else's pace. Learning to read has its leaps forward and its sudden retreats, its periods of hunger and its long doldrums with no appetite. We need to recognize how individuals evolve as readers and support them on their journey so they can begin to see themselves as capable readers.

Of course, this set of theoretical principles is not exhaustive, and most people would probably add one or two new ones to those presented here. For example, one might add that teaching is an art, or that teachers must be reflective about their practice, or that education is a highly political endeavor, and so forth. However, the ten theoretical principles about teaching reading that I have provided here establish an evidence-based foundation for developing an effective reading workshop. It is my hope that this book will help teachers envision how digital and web-based resources can be used to enhance their reading workshops and provide support for selecting those tools and approaches that support readers in the digital era through the reading workshop 2.0 framework.

CHAPTER

The Reading Workshop Revisited

*We must welcome the future, remembering that soon it will
be the past; and we must respect the past, remembering that it
was once all that was possible.*

—George Santayana, 2009

The primary challenge when writing this book was to avoid giving the impression that I am discarding all the work I've done previously on the reading workshop, while not repeating everything I've written in my other books and articles. As the opening epigraph suggests, others have wrestled with similar challenges. As reading teachers it is important to remember where we have been in order to have a better sense of where we are headed. The reading workshop 2.0 framework described in this book is built upon similar theoretical and pedagogical foundations provided in my first book *The Reading Workshop: Creating Space for Readers* (Serafini 2001) and expanded upon in *Around the Reading Workshop in 180 Days: A Month-by-Month Guide to Effective Instruction* (Serafini and Youngs 2006). I highly recommend these two resources for a more comprehensive explanation of my vision for the reading workshop.

In this book I am extending the discussion of what I think are the most effective instructional approaches for developing successful readers into digital and web-based environments. I have erred on the side of brevity in revisiting my previous ideas so that I can emphasize the pedagogical strands and instructional components that support readers in the digital age. This chapter serves as a reminder of my past so that together we can build a better reading workshop 2.0 framework for the future.

Looking back on the challenges I faced as a classroom teacher when I was working on my first book about the reading workshop, I wrote the following in the opening chapter:

> *One of the biggest challenges for me in designing my reading workshop is to create a framework that supports children's development as readers and provides a consistent, predictable environment that allows children to be successful. Consistency is an important aspect of the reading workshop; however, I don't want our routines to become tedious and uninspiring. The structures I put in place need to free children to be creative, to allow them to read and explore new texts, and to experience the joys of children's literature. (2001, 7–8)*

To this day, I completely agree with this statement that I penned over fifteen years ago. I believe that consistency is still an important consideration in developing a reading workshop, and that the procedures and routines we establish should support the literate development of young readers without curbing their imaginations or enjoyment as readers. Time spent developing effective classroom environments, setting appropriate expectations, and establishing a community of readers all provide a solid foundation for teachers' reading instruction approaches.

Many changes have taken place since I wrote *The Reading Workshop: Creating Space for Readers* in 2001. The challenges we face today as reading teachers have expanded with the introduction of digital and web-based texts, resources, and environments. They include changes in the formats and types of texts available, in the strategies readers need to make sense of complex texts, in the instructional practices promoted in schools, and, most importantly, in my own understanding of reading and reading instruction.

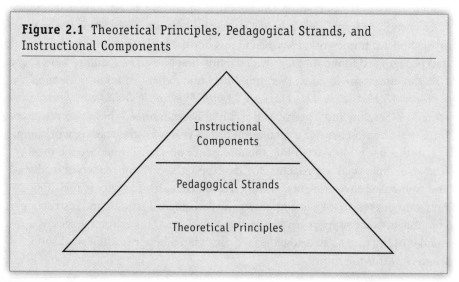

Figure 2.1 Theoretical Principles, Pedagogical Strands, and Instructional Components

Instructional Components

Pedagogical Strands

Theoretical Principles

In this chapter I begin by defining, in general, what I consider to be a framework for implementing a reading workshop. Next, I revisit the pedagogical strands that formed the foundation of my original reading workshop framework and how they connect to the new framework. Finally, I will describe the instructional components that make up the day-to-day learning experiences of my new reading workshop 2.0 framework. These pedagogical strands and instructional components form the instructional framework for the reading workshop 2.0. In Figure 2.1, a pyramid formation provides a metaphor for the relationship among principles, strands, and components. The instructional components are built upon the foundation of pedagogical strands, which are in turn based on the theoretical principles delineated in Chapter 1.

The Reading Workshop Defined

The reading workshop is not a program that comes with a predetermined script, nor is it a scope and sequence of individual lessons. Instead, it is an organizational framework that provides routines and procedures to support the instructional approaches and components described later in this chapter. It is also an instructional framework for locating reading instruction. Reading instruction takes place across different settings and contexts, not simply when the teacher is standing in front of the room. The reading workshop framework organizes a wide array of learning experiences to help teachers support children at their individual points of need.

The reading workshop also creates a space for both teacher-student and student-student interactions. Students are given time to engage with authentic texts for authentic purposes and time to share their thinking with other members of a community of readers. The reading workshop is as much a social network as it is a physical space. Attention must be paid to the ways in which we organize the physical objects and resources in our classrooms as well as the social interactions that take place in these spaces.

As outlined in my two previous books on the reading workshop, the experiences that I provide in *Reading Workshop 2.0* are a blend of *preplanned engagements* and *response-centered instructional approaches*. I don't go into the reading workshop 2.0 any more unprepared than I went into my original reading workshop. However, I also don't go in unwilling to adapt the learning experiences and resources I provide for addressing the needs and interests of my readers. The ability to provide learning experiences that support children's development as sophisticated readers, the willingness to take advantage of the *teachable moment* when it arises, and the requisite knowledge base needed to respond to the day-to-day interactions in the reading workshop 2.0 are important considerations for creating an effective workshop framework.

Pedagogical Strands

The four strands described in this section provide the pedagogical foundation upon which the instructional components of the reading workshop 2.0 framework are founded. These pedagogical strands weave back and forth across my theoretical principles, available resources, and the day-to-day learning experiences I design. The four pedagogical strands are (1) opportunity, (2) choice, (3) response, and (4) community.

These strands have been developed through my own research, teaching experiences, and the readings of other giants in the field of literacy education, in particular Nancie Atwell, Frank Smith, Ralph Peterson, Lucy Calkins, P. David Pearson, Louise Rosenblatt, Ken Goodman, and many others. It is on the shoulders of these educational giants that these pedagogical strands have evolved.

Pedagogical Strand #1: Opportunity

Providing opportunities for children to read, browse, talk, share, and explore a variety of texts is the basis of engagement. Without opportunities to engage with texts, children will never develop as readers. As Frank Smith (1988) suggested, readers learn to read by reading. However, without opportunities to access a wide variety of texts and time to explore them, they would never have the chance to engage in the act of reading. To become a successful reader one must have multiple opportunities to read, access to many types of texts, comfortable spaces to read and talk, and support for selecting appropriate things to read.

Opportunity as a pedagogical strand has three dimensions: (1) access, (2) time, and (3) space. Although each of these three dimensions is important, all three dimensions are necessary to provide authentic opportunities for children to develop as readers. Only by providing all three dimensions can we offer our students opportunities to become readers.

Access to a wide range of relevant, interesting things to read is the first dimension for providing opportunities for children to develop as readers. Not only do we as classroom teachers need to create expansive classroom libraries, we need to take advantage of all the texts available in our schools, communities, and online. Access must extend beyond the four walls of the classroom.

In our classrooms, we need to organize our book collections to make them inviting and accessible. Displaying book covers along the classroom walls—not just the spines on bookshelves—that feature what is being read and discussed in literary displays like those found in contemporary bookstores and providing access to high-quality reading materials are paramount for providing access to the texts and resources needed to develop children as readers.

I have long been a proponent of extensive public and school libraries, and I remain so to this day. However, I know that proximity to reading materials has to be closer than across town or even across campus. When it's time to read, children need things to read that are within arm's length. Just like access to reading materials provided in the doctor's office or magazines placed in the back pocket of an airplane seat, readers need to be able to reach over without even getting up to grab their texts when it's time to read.

With the advent of digital and web-based resources, access to reading materials has changed dramatically. After finishing one book on a digital reading device or computer, children can quickly search through related titles and get recommendations from other readers before instantly downloading another book. The libraries and bookstores of the world become available to readers as long as they have an Internet connection.

I have books scattered throughout my home, all for different purposes, to be read at different times and in different places. Books on my bedside table serve a different purpose from the magazines on my coffee table or the professional books that line the shelves in my office. If we read differently at different times in different places, so do our students; therefore, we must provide them the same access and opportunities we give ourselves. The variety of reading materials we provide our readers needs to range across topics, length, genre, reading levels, and modes of delivery.

Time is the second dimension of the opportunity strand—time to read, time to share ideas, time to wonder, and time to explore new texts. We cannot master something we don't dedicate our time to, it's just that simple. For children to develop as proficient and sophisticated readers they need time to work through all the facets, challenges, and possibilities of what it means to be a reader. They need time to explore the various strategies we demonstrate in our lessons and time to make sense of the complex texts they encounter.

In essence, children need to find time in their lives to become readers. As busy as their lives are, I often wonder when they will have time to settle down and read something. I know that even in my life as a children's literature professor I find it hard to read as much as I would like. The challenge is one of prioritizing. We give time to those things we like and those things in which we find value. One of the biggest challenges we face as reading teachers is providing ample time during the school day for reading, as well as helping students find time in their busy lives outside of school to read enough to develop as proficient and sophisticated readers.

Space is the final dimension in the opportunity strand that we need to consider. We always read some particular text, in some particular place, for some particular reason. There are spaces to sit and read; spaces to share what has been read; spaces to browse and explore new books, magazines, and everything else available; and spaces to engage in book discussions—simply put, spaces to do all those things readers do.

One way to approach this is to consider the types of spaces we provide for ourselves as readers and how can we bring these spaces into our classrooms. For example, I know that I wouldn't sit for hours on a hard plastic chair in a corner of my house to read a novel; maybe we should stop asking our children to do so as well. When it's time for me to sit and read at home, I choose my favorite reading chair where I have my reading lamp, I put on some smooth jazz music, get some tea or sparkling water and maybe a light snack, and sit back and engage in a novel, professional book, or magazine for hours. I wish I could offer my students all the comforts I offer myself.

Classroom reading areas, comfortable chairs, soft music, headphones for isolation, and pillows all help create spaces that foster engagement and help readers sustain reading for longer periods of time. We may not be able to bring in couches and reading lamps—let alone scones, jazz music, and tea—but we have to consider how we organize the spaces in our classrooms and how they support or detract from our goal of developing lifelong readers.

Pedagogical Strand #2: Choice

The next pedagogical strand involves the process of choosing what to read. As adult readers, one of the basic rights we allow ourselves is the right to choose what we read. The process of choosing signals one's ownership of the act of reading. Having spent time talking to many young readers over the past twenty years, one of their biggest complaints about reading in school has always been they don't get to pick what they read. This has to change if we are to help children become lifelong readers.

Choice is contingent upon providing the types of access and opportunity explained in the first strand. Readers don't have real choices without having access to a wide variety of texts. We can tell readers to go ahead and select any text they want, but if only a few books are available the choice is not real. Thirty children in a classroom selecting from a small library of one hundred books doesn't really equal choice. The National Council of Teachers of English and the American Library Association have recommended having upwards of one hundred books per reader in our classrooms if we are to foster a real sense of choice. Continuous access to classroom, school, home, and public libraries is necessary if we are to approach these numbers.

To develop children as lifelong, independent readers they need to take ownership of their reading lives. The most important first step in doing so is allowing them to choose what they read. Sometimes we provide choices within a particular framework; for example, all my students may be asked to read a book of historical fiction at some point in the school year. However, within that genre they are free to choose whichever historical fiction text intrigues them most.

And to support readers' choices we have to give them insight into what texts are available, or what I call *supportive browsing*. Too often, the children who struggle the most as readers are those who do not have a deep understanding of what they have to choose from. To support them as they browse, we need to keep current with the latest and greatest selections of children's literature. We have to conduct numerous book talks every day; interview students to find out what types of texts interest them; explore strategies for selecting high-quality, compelling texts; allow children to share their favorite selections with other readers; and take advantage of web-based and digital resources for providing recommendations for what is currently available.

For example, when I buy a new book on Amazon, the website automatically generates numerous recommendations. Because I buy many books on Amazon, I am offered and made aware of many other possible texts to explore. The more I read and explore, the more the world opens up to me about what is available. It's the same for the readers in our classrooms. Those who spend time reading and exploring books in the library and online are better positioned to know what is available to read and are more likely to find something they like or need. We cannot leave our readers adrift, hoping they'll find something to read. We as teachers need to support their browsing to help make it more effective and efficient for them.

Pedagogical Strand #3: Response

If opportunity and choice are the basic elements of engagement, response is the basic element of teaching. Through our responses to readers' efforts and thinking, we demonstrate the strategies they will need to comprehend the texts they read, set expectations for what we hope they will achieve, introduce them to more complex texts, and help them envision themselves as readers.

Our children come to see themselves as readers through our eyes as well as their own. When we talk to them and label them as struggling readers, they learn to see themselves in that light. How we respond to our students makes a big difference in how they see themselves as readers. It helps them understand what the act of reading is really about and us to see how they respond to the instructional experiences we provide.

Teaching children to read is part demonstrating what reading is and how readers do it, and part responding to children's efforts when they themselves engage in the act of reading. As teachers, we demonstrate what proficient, sophisticated readers do when they engage with various texts, and then we invite them to try out what we have shown them. Our demonstrations range from showing readers how to select an appropriate text, to navigating textual and hypertextual elements, to generating interpretations, and to discussing and analyzing what has been read. These demonstrations provide invitations for our readers to take on the strategies and practices associated with proficient reading.

As readers work to develop their own strategies, we guide them through the process, scaffolding their attempts through our responses to their efforts. We draw upon our assessments to come to know our children as readers and to help us respond to their efforts and guide our instructional decisions. In this way, teaching children to read is more about responding to what they are trying to do than developing elaborate minilessons to perform in front of the classroom. We have to pay as much attention to the readers in our classrooms as we do to the curriculum guides we are often required to follow.

Pedagogical Strand #4: Community

We learn from the company we keep, it's that simple. Our parents knew this, so they worried about the friends we made and the company we kept as we grew up. In our classrooms, it's no different. If we want our children to become readers, they have to spend time in the company of other readers. They have to see themselves as readers like the people around them. And they have to have the same resources, spaces, and opportunities that other successful readers have available to them.

A community of readers is a group of children that shares the common goal of learning to read, reading and discussing literature, and becoming literate human beings. This community is built upon mutual respect and willingness on the part of each participant to listen and consider the merits of each member's ideas and interpretations. A community of readers is a dynamic entity that develops over the course of the school year, changes as events take place and children come and go, and requires teachers' attention if it is to evolve into an effective support for children's development as readers. In effect, this community of readers is a model of the kind of world we want to live in.

The rituals we create in our classrooms help to foster a sense of community among our children. Morning messages and opening ceremonies help children start their day by sharing their own lives and ideas and by listening to the lives and ideas of others. If we want children to openly and honestly share what they think about a book we have just read aloud, we need to make them feel comfortable talking with other children throughout the day.

By setting clear and obtainable expectations for our readers, we help them to understand what we want them to do as readers. The rituals, procedures, and expectations that are established during the beginning of the school year set the tone for the reading workshop. Children rise to our expectations, so we need to establish appropriate, obtainable expectations for the types of readers we want to develop in our classroom community.

Reading is as much a social act as it is a private one. The language used in the texts we read was developed in our culture long before we came to these texts. The meanings associated or connected to that shared language were also developed and continue to evolve in social contexts. To support students' development as readers, we have to show them how readers act, how they talk about books, how to disagree without offending anyone, how to complete their response logs, how to choose a new book, and many other social practices necessary for being a successful reader in our classrooms.

Instructional Components of the Reading Workshop 2.0

The six instructional components of the reading workshop are assembled upon the platform provided by the theoretical principles and pedagogical strands (see Figure 2.2). These instructional components are more practical in scope and intention than the theoretical principles and pedagogical strands. They represent the array of day-to-day learning experiences I have provided in my reading workshops throughout the years. At this time I don't see the need to add any additional instructional components to my original framework. Rather, I see the reading workshop 2.0 framework as simply an expansion of the existing instructional components, using new web-based and digital resources in their implementation. The principles, strands, and instructional components associated with the reading workshop 2.0 framework address the constantly evolving nature of what is being read and the strategies needed to make sense of more complex, multimodal texts.

In the following section I will briefly describe what each instructional component entails and then offer resources, which I have created previously, for further exploration. In fact, I have written professional development books and articles that address each of these components individually and will share these and other resources with you as we move forward.

Establishing a Literate Environment

There are two important aspects to consider when working to establish an effective literate environment: (1) *the physical environment*—classroom resources, organization, and procedures—and (2) *the social environment*—the roles of the teacher and students within a community of readers, the type of talk that takes place, and the rituals and expectations that are established. The literate environment that we develop in our classrooms has a profound impact on how children

---

Figure 2.2 The Six Instructional Components of a Reading Workshop 2.0 Framework

- A Literate Environment
- Reading Aloud
- Interactive Discussions
- Intensive and Extensive Reading
- Lessons in Comprehension
- Literacy Assessment

---

see themselves as readers. Learning to read is as much a part of seeing oneself or identifying oneself as a reader as it is enacting any particular reading strategies. The physical and social spaces, time allocations, and the sense of community we develop need to have particular attention paid to them if they are to be positive supports for our children's development as readers.

Professional Resources:

Chapter 3 in Serafini, Frank. 2001. *The Reading Workshop: Creating Space for Readers*. Portsmouth, NH: Heinemann.

Chapter 2 in Serafini, Frank, and Suzette Youngs. 2006. *Around the Reading Workshop in 180 Days: A Month-by-Month Guide to Effective Instruction*. Portsmouth, NH: Heinemann.

Chapter 2 in Serafini, Frank. 2009. *Interactive Comprehension Strategies: Fostering Meaningful Talk About Text*. New York: Scholastic.

Chapters 3 and 5 in Serafini, Frank, and Cyndi Giorgis. 2003. *Reading Aloud and Beyond: Fostering the Intellectual Life with Older Readers*. Portsmouth, NH: Heinemann.

Reading Aloud with Children

At the beginning of the year I focus on establishing the read-aloud as a daily ritual and setting expectations for students during this event. There is no instructional approach that is more effective or efficient than reading aloud with children. You may notice I use the term *with* here to describe what I intend by this event. I think we *read along with* readers, not simply *at* them. The readers in my classrooms are co-creators of the read-aloud event. They participate by paying attention, asking questions, offering opinions and interpretations, and selecting what to read next. I simply give a voice to the story or informational text being read so that the readers in my classroom can listen, engage, and enjoy.

Professional Resources:

Serafini, Frank, and Cyndi Giorgis. 2003. *Reading Aloud and Beyond: Fostering the Intellectual Life with Older Readers*. Portsmouth, NH: Heinemann.

Campbell, Robin. 2001. *Read-Alouds with Young Children*. Newark, DE: International Reading Association.

Fox, Mem. 2001. *Reading Magic: Why Reading Aloud to Our Children Will Change Their Lives Forever*. San Diego: Harcourt Brace.

Trelease, Jim. 1989. *The New Read-Aloud Handbook*. New York: Penguin.

Facilitating Interactive Discussions

The quality of the discussions that take place in the read-aloud set the stage for the quality of the discussions we will have in our literature study groups. The level of sophistication of our small-group literature studies is contingent upon the quality of the whole-group discussions we have after a read-aloud. The demonstrations, both intended and unintended, that we offer students during our read-aloud and discussions support the quality of the thinking–talking that will occur in other settings.

Professional Resources:

Serafini, Frank. 2009. *Interactive Comprehension Strategies: Fostering Meaningful Talk About Text*. New York: Scholastic.

Myhill, Debra, Susan Jones, and Rosemary Hopper. 2006. *Talking, Listening, Learning: Effective Talk in the Primary Classroom*. Berkshire, England: Open University Press.

Nystrand, Martin. 1997. *Opening Dialogue: Understanding the Dynamics of Language and Learning in the English Classroom*. New York: Teachers College Press.

Supporting Intensive and Extensive Reading

One of the primary considerations early in the year in the reading workshop is establishing procedures that allow students to work independently, developing their own reading practices and proficiencies. This frees up the teacher to work with individuals or with readers in small groups. For example, learning how to find and select an appropriate text is an important factor in supporting extensive reading. Other ways of supporting extensive reading include: assessing readers to determine appropriate selections for them; providing space for personal collections, or *book baskets*, for students to organize future reading materials; implementing response journals to hold readers accountable for reading; and reducing extrinsic reward systems to keep the focus on the value and importance of reading in and of itself.

Intensive reading is associated with literature study groups or classroom book clubs (Peterson and Eeds 1990). In these small groups, readers gather together to discuss what they have read with other interested readers. Sharing one's ideas and experiences of reading the same novel, picture book, informational text, or other text is important for readers to develop their abilities to articulate their ideas, interpret what has been read, and consider the ideas and opinions of other readers. In these small groups, teachers serve as *literary docents*, helping readers navigate the books they select, challenging them to reconsider initial interpretations, and supporting deeper analyses of what they have experienced.

Professional Resources:

Miller, Donalyn. 2009. *The Book Whisperer: Awakening the Inner Reader in Every Child*. San Francisco: Jossey-Bass.

Peterson, Ralph, and Maryann Eeds. 1990. *Grand Conversations: Literature Groups in Action*. New York: Scholastic.

Wilde, Sandra. 2013. *Quantity and Quality: Increasing the Volume and Complexity of Students' Reading*. Portsmouth, NH: Heinemann.

Developing Lessons in Comprehension

Teachers help readers learn to read by demonstrating what proficient and sophisticated readers do, helping them to understand what strategies will help with particular texts and tasks. They provide support as readers begin to take on these strategies and reading practices by creating time and space for students to apply them. These learning experiences are all aspects of quality lessons in comprehension.

Although comprehension instruction is often thought of as when a teacher lectures in front of a classroom, comprehension lessons actually take place throughout the entire reading workshop. When teachers work alongside students, helping them use different strategies to understand a text or explaining the criteria successful readers use to choose an appropriate text for independent reading, they are teaching comprehension. This said, there are times in the reading workshop when I do stand in front of my students for a brief period of time to demonstrate particular strategies for comprehending texts or procedures to be followed in the reading workshop. Effective lessons in comprehension are explicit, deliberate, preplanned instructional experiences designed to help readers develop their ability to read.

Professional Resources:

Serafini, Frank. 2004. *Lessons in Comprehension: Explicit Instruction in the Reading Workshop*. Portsmouth, NH: Heinemann.

Serafini, Frank, and Suzette Youngs. 2008. *More (Advanced) Lessons in Comprehension: Expanding Students' Understanding of All Types of Texts*. Portsmouth, NH: Heinemann.

Assessing Children as Readers

The assessment practices I use are based on my understandings of what I consider to be important aspects of being a reader. I gather information through a variety of assessment *windows* to compile a more complete picture of my students as readers. Assessment is always *selective* and *partial*. It is through many different assessment instruments that this picture begins to evolve.

In contrast to the challenges of standardized, external assessments, classroom-based assessments provide information that can be used to support students' learning and development. These assessments need to be *efficient*, meaning they do not require tremendous amounts of time, and *effective*, meaning they provide the information teachers need to drive curricular decisions. In addition, classroom-based assessments take place over time, are noncompetitive, are grounded in authentic acts of reading, and focus on readers' strengths rather than their deficits. They provide teachers with the information necessary for making day-to-day instructional decisions.

Traditionally, assessment has been viewed as something we do *to* students rather than *with* students. Too often, classroom teachers give readers tests, score them, and later explain to them how they did. Learning stopped as assessment occurred, and students were often left in the dark as to their progress. Portfolios, student-led conferences, learning logs, and negotiated reporting ideas may all help to include the student in the assessment process.

Professional Resource:

Serafini, Frank. 2010a. *Classroom Reading Assessments: More Efficient Ways to View and Evaluate Your Readers.* Portsmouth, NH: Heinemann.

Some Additional Thoughts

The instructional components of the reading workshop described in this chapter are framed by the pedagogical strands outlined previously, which in turn are based on the theoretical principles outlined in Chapter 1. All three elements— principles, strands, and components—are important aspects of the reading workshop. When asked about the kinds of things that actually happen in my reading workshop, I usually answer by sharing the six instructional components listed here, rather than expounding on the pedagogical strands or theoretical principles. The instructional components are more practical in scope; however, all of these elements are essential for developing an effective reading workshop framework. The instructional components for the reading workshop must be grounded in sound theoretical principles and supported by the pedagogical strands presented here if they are to serve the primary goal of changing the way teachers and students think and talk about texts. The instructional components are the day-to-day practices through which the pedagogical strands and theoretical principles are brought to life in the reading workshop.

CHAPTER THREE

Making the Shift to Reading Workshop 2.0

Many researchers have identified the "old wine in new bottles" syndrome, whereby long-standing school literacy routines have a new technology tacked on here or there, without in any way changing the substance of the practice.

—Colin Lankshear and Michelle Knobel, 2006

From the outset of this book, I have suggested that the changes associated with a shift from a reading workshop 1.0 to a reading workshop 2.0 framework are better conceptualized as *evolutionary* rather than *revolutionary*. The changes presented in this book do not amount to a complete overhaul of my original framework; rather, they are an extension of my original work into the digital era. In either a 1.0 or 2.0 reading workshop framework, readers still need to learn to select appropriate texts, decode written language, consider visual images and graphic designs, discuss ideas, and analyze texts for meaning potential. Similarly, teachers still need to read aloud to children, facilitate interactive discussions, provide demonstrations of reading strategies, support intensive and extensive reading, and assess the readers in their classrooms. How new resources and technologies can support the shift from a reading workshop 1.0 to a reading workshop 2.0 framework is the question this book is designed to answer.

Although the theoretical principles about teaching reading, the pedagogical strands, and the essential instructional components that form the foundation of both the reading workshop 1.0 and the reading workshop 2.0 frameworks remain basically the same, the resources, texts, and lessons have been adapted to take advantage of the web-based and digital resources available to us as reading teachers. As we reconsider the instructional approaches and learning experiences provided in a reading workshop 1.0 environment, we have to learn how to take advantage of the web-based and digital resources available to us as classroom teachers to support our readers in the digital age.

A Brief Vignette

A few years ago while visiting my sister Suzette and her family, my then twelve-year-old niece, Chandler, said she was going downstairs to read *The Hunger Games* by Suzanne Collins (2008) with her friends. I assumed, quite incorrectly, that her friends were gathered together in the basement, holding copies of the book and sharing parts of it as they read aloud to one another and discussed events in the story. I could not have been more wrong.

When I went downstairs later to see what was happening, I saw Chandler sitting by herself in front of her laptop computer. A digital version of the book was open on one side of the screen and a window to Skype video communications software was open on the other side displaying the face of one of her friends. They were simultaneously reading a digital version of the book on their digital reading devices while chatting about the story over Skype, highlighting the text and posting comments through some software application. In addition, Chandler was typing on her smartphone so she could text-message a third friend who did not have access to her laptop that evening but wanted to read along with her friends. When they finished reading a particular section of the book, they agreed to go onto Goodreads.com to post their latest commentaries in a Hunger Games chatroom they had joined earlier. After reading each section, they went online to visit the author's website. There they looked for some clues the author might have shared in an interview about her motives for writing the book.

At that moment I fully realized how much things around reading had changed since I was in the classroom and would continue to change in the future. Even though Chandler and her friends were simply reading a novel together, the digital and web-based resources available to support their reading, discussions, interpretations, and analysis had changed everything. The resources available when I wrote *The Reading Workshop: Creating Space for Readers* in 2001 pale in comparison to what is available to teachers and students nowadays. I realized a new book about the reading workshop was absolutely necessary.

What Is Web 2.0 All About?

According to Davies and Merchant (2009), the changing nature of online engagement—often referred to as Web 2.0—privileges interaction over information. In a Web 2.0 environment, digital and web-based resources promote social interaction, collaboration, and user-generated content. These resources have changed notions of copyright, authorship, dissemination, advertising, and what it means to be literate in the twenty-first century. O'Reilly (2005) used the term *Web 2.0*, from which the term *Reading Workshop 2.0* was adapted, to signify the evolution of web-based resources and applications from an information-gathering system to an interactive platform. In a Web 2.0 environment, users *generate* content as well as *search* through institutionally generated content. Web 2.0 represents both a change in the technical aspects of various web-based and digital resources as well as a change in the social practices and networks associated with these new technologies. Although children in school may be asked to research content on Wikipedia.com, they rarely if ever are expected to add content, look through the history of the page's development, or revise various pages. Generating content in addition to searching for information takes advantage of the interactive, social, and collaborative nature of various web-based platforms in a Web 2.0 environment.

In the opening epigraph, Lankshear and Knobel (2006) cautioned us to consider what they have referred to as the "old wine in new bottles" syndrome (54). Davies and Merchant (2009) referred to the same phenomenon as "technologically polished performances of conventional literacy practices" (2). In both cases, these expressions refer to doing the same old thing in the name of literacy education but simply doing it online or on a tablet instead of with paper and pencil. Having students create a book report using presentation software such as PowerPoint or Prezi or having students upload questions generated during a read-aloud to a website like Edmodo is simply doing the same old thing with new technologies. A book report is still a book report even if it appears on a screen, and a list of questions is simply a list of questions even if it is sent to an educational website.

Information and communication technologies focus on new means of facilitating communication, not simply new technologies. Just as changing social practices associated with information and communication have supported changes in technologies, changes in technologies have supported changes in those social practices. Reading and writing are cultural practices, not just technological proficiencies. We learn to read and write and partake in these practices because we are members of a culture, and these practices support our lives as literate beings (Newkirk 2012).

Lankshear and Knobel (2006) suggest that Web 2.0 resources and environments involve three interlocking features or practices: (1) participation, (2) collaboration, and (3) dissemination. These features represent a change in worldview as much as an upgrade in available technologies; it's *how* these technologies are used that signals the changes to which they are referring. The changes in technologies have evolved because of the changing nature of society and how we communicate.

According to Davies and Merchant (2009), compared to Web 1.0 resources, Web 2.0 resources presuppose a more active user who is encouraged to design an online presence and participate in a community of like-minded users. Where Web 1.0 resources position readers as passive consumers of information, Web 2.0 resources presuppose a more active, collaborative, and participatory stance for readers.

Additionally, Web 2.0 applications and platforms gather as much information about the user as the user learns about the content presented and shared. Websites use *cookies* and other web-based technologies to gather information about the sites we visit, the purchases we make, the websites we bookmark, the social networks we subscribe to, and the content we post online.

We use the Internet to learn more about the world while institutions, companies, and advertisers learn more about our interests and our lives. It seems that the distinctions among producers and consumers, users and advertisers, and institutions and individuals will be forever blurred.

Davies and Merchant (2009) proffered four key characteristics of Web 2.0 experiences and resources. These characteristics include:

1. Presence: Users of Web 2.0 are active participants, creating avatars and profiles for communicating with others.

2. Modification: The interfaces we use in Web 2.0 applications are modifiable to suit users' needs and preferences.

3. User-generated content: Platforms like wikis, blogs, and podcasts allow users to generate and disseminate content.

4. Social participation: Web 2.0 resources provide invitations to participate in technologically mediated social practices.

In Web 2.0 environments, readers are positioned as active readers, adding content to what is already available, modifying the profiles and platforms they use, and participating in *affinity spaces* with others with similar interests and experiences (Gee and Hayes 2011). The aforementioned changes that have taken place in the roles readers assume, the resources available to us as classroom teachers, and the complexity of the texts being read and created are important to consider as we evolve into a reading workshop 2.0 framework.

What Shifts Are Occurring?

To get a sense of the various shifts that have occurred and those I have described throughout this chapter, take a minute and fill out the chart in Figure 3.1 before reading further. I have completed the first row to give you a sense of my purpose for completing this activity. The purpose of this chart is to consider the changes in technology associated with particular everyday experiences and the benefits and challenges that may arise.

Figure 3.1 Comparing New and Traditional Technologies

Literate Event or Social Practice	Traditional Technologies	New Technologies	Benefits of New Technologies	Challenges with New Technologies
Visual Entertainment	Go to the movies.	Stream videos on tablet. Buy movies online.	Immediate access. More portable. Done in home.	Not as social. Smaller screens = less impact.
Personal Communication				
Advertising Products				
Listening to Music				

You can see from Figure 3.1 that there are benefits and challenges associated with every change in technology. Not all changes in technology have led to positive changes in our lives and social interactions. Educators and researchers have documented the negative effects of living online (Rosen 2012; Turkle 2011) and the new social mores associated with living in a participatory culture (Jenkins, Ford, and Green 2013). As these technologies and the social practices associated with them continue to play a larger and larger role in our lives and our students' lives, we must consider how these changes affect our development as literate beings.

To contextualize this discussion about changing resources, social practices, and learning environments, I will present a series of three *shifts* that help explain and elaborate the changes we face as literacy educators today. These shifts are: (1) theoretical, (2) pedagogical, and (3) textual. Each shift focuses on different dimensions of the reading workshop 2.0 framework and should be considered as we develop our preferred vision for the instructional practices in our classrooms (see Figures 3.2, 3.3, and 3.4).

These theoretical, pedagogical, and textual shifts have occurred because of new technologies and new social practices that have been supported by these rapidly changing technologies. As teachers, we face many challenges as literacy educators in the new millennium. As definitions of what it means to be literate change from autonomous models—where being literate is defined as the accumulation of individual skills and competencies—to social models—where being literate means the ability to perform certain actions, roles, and identities in a variety of contexts—so too must our pedagogies change to support these new definitions.

Figure 3.2 Theoretical Shifts

- From Web 1.0 (focus on consumption) to Web 2.0 (focus on interaction)
- From autonomous models of literacy to social models of literacies
- From websites providing information to social media platforms supporting collaboration
- From in-class communities of readers to global communities of readers
- From institutionally generated content to user-generated content

Figure 3.3 Pedagogical Shifts

- From teacher as transmitter of knowledge to teacher as co-learner
- From reading slowly and deeply to skimming and navigating vast amounts of text
- From sharing interpretations with classmates to participating in online discussions with readers from around the world
- From putting sticky notes in novels to using digital highlighting and commentary tools
- From print-based literature response notebooks to reader-designed blogs and social networking sites

Figure 3.4 Textual Shifts

- From print-based to web-based and digital texts
- From written language texts (monomodal) to texts with images, design elements, sound effects, video clips, and graphic elements (multimodal)
- From reading paths set by the designer to reading paths set by the reader
- From ink-based texts that are permanent and inflexible to digital texts that can be altered by size, font, and orientation
- From bold headings to hypertextual links

As the texts that readers encounter evolve into multimodal ensembles (Serafini 2014), the instructional approaches and lessons we provide need to evolve to address the nature of these complex texts. Multimodal texts represent radical changes from the traditional texts that have been a staple in classrooms for the past fifty years (Dresang 1999). These complex texts comprise interactive features, hyperlinks, visual images, and sound effects, and they require readers to bring a variety of strategies and an expanded interpretive repertoire to comprehend and make use of them.

What Are Web 2.0 Literacies?

There are many terms associated with Web 2.0 literacies: *new literacies*, *multiliteracies*, *digital literacies*, *twenty-first-century literacies*, *web-based literacies*, *ICT literacies*, and *techno-literacies* are just some of the terms I have come across in my research for this book. The term I use most frequently to describe the changes taking place is *multiliteracies*. This term was first used by the New London Group (1996) in their manifesto outlining the changes they foresaw coming in the later part of the twentieth century.

Multiliteracies refers to the reconceptualization of literacy as a multidimensional set of competences and social practices in response to the increasing complexity and multimodal nature of texts. Visual literacy, media literacy, critical literacy, computer literacy, and other types of literacies are brought together under this umbrella term to suggest the need to expand the concept of literacy beyond reading and writing print-based texts. As the texts that readers encounter grow in complexity, in both print and digital forms, the literacies required to navigate, interpret, design, and analyze these texts also grows in complexity (Serafini 2012b).

In addition to new social practices and definitions of literacy, Web 2.0 literacies involve new forms of technology. Pencil-and-paper technologies associated with traditional forms of literacy are transformed in the digital age to the mouse, the smartphone, and the computer screen. Some of the digital resources, software platforms, and web-based applications used to search and navigate the Internet, collaborate with others, and share content are listed in Figure 3.5.

We live in a technologically mediated world (Boyd 2014). This means our lives are mediated by the social interactions and technologies we use to go about our daily routines. Our methods of communication, our access to information, how we share what we have learned, and how we interact with one another are mediated by the digital tools available in school and at home. It seems the Internet has become a conduit through which all information and communication flows.

Becoming more comfortable with the various technologies available to us in the digital age is important as we consider our careers, families, friends, and other aspects of our lives. However, familiarity with the latest technological

Figure 3.5 Digital and Web-Based Resources

- Social media
- Weblogs
- Streaming video
- Podcasts
- Wikis
- Websites
- Interactive apps
- Social bookmarks
- Photo-sharing platforms

gadgets or web-based services is often less important than possessing the critical knowledge to engage productively with networked situations (Boyd 2014). Familiarity alone is not enough to meet the demands placed upon our children and ourselves for being fully literate as we move into the new millennium. Our children will not only need help accessing and using these new resources, they will also need help learning to critically analyze the content and resources made available in today's digital environments.

Even though social and entertainment-based literacies—including social networking sites, photo-sharing platforms, video games, and text-messaging—are common practices among readers in many of our classes, using web-based and digital resources as tools for educational purposes such as conducting research, writing on a weblog, or developing a multimodal presentation are not part of their daily experiences (Asselin and Moayeri 2011). The students in our class may be able to update their Facebook accounts and send text messages, but they usually don't understand how these platforms work, nor do many of them have the experiences necessary for adapting them to specific learning experiences.

Web-based and digital resources are dynamic, user-centered, interactive, collaborative, democratic, and support online communities (Joosten 2012). These resources have the potential to increase interactions among individuals by providing spaces and platforms for sharing content and opinions. As these digital and web-based tools play a more extensive role in our lives, we must learn to navigate the social and literacy practices that mediate our lives and our educational experiences.

Some Additional Thoughts

Too often, teachers ask their students to "power down" upon entering their school or classrooms (Ormiston 2011), to turn off their smartphones, tablets, laptops, and digital reading devices. Yet outside of school, children's lives are connected to one another through these various technologies. What's more, inside school they are often asked to sit in rows where talking may be considered some form of cheating. If technology supports increased engagement and collaboration outside of schools, then logically teachers should be able to use it in classrooms to support engagement and collaboration in their learning experiences.

Unfortunately, children often use more advanced technologies in their homes on a daily basis compared to what they have available and are allowed to use in schools. This is an unfortunate scenario given the demands placed upon today's youth. The more we ask them to go back to outdated, traditional literacy practices, the less visible their literate abilities in school will become. Lack of opportunities to participate in the digitally mediated social practices available to other, more affluent peers is a damaging form of exclusion. The chasm of the digital divide between haves and have-nots must be bridged if we are to help all learners be literate in the twenty-first century (Castells 2002).

Readers in today's classrooms are often referred to as *digital natives* (Prensky 2001). This term refers to children who have been exposed to digital and web-based technologies since birth, compared to *digital immigrants*, which refers to those who have experienced the changes from analog to digital in their lifetime. This second group, the digital immigrants, includes most of the teachers with whom I work. Making the shift from using predominantly Web 1.0 resources to incorporating web-based and digital web 2.0 resources is a major challenge for many teachers, young and old. Finding ways to take advantage of not only the new bottles but also the new wine can be invigorating, yet challenging at the same time.

In the digital age, reading is no longer simply decoding printed text. Instead, it is a complex process that entails a variety of social practices used for making sense of the more complex and multimodal texts encountered in today's world. This includes making sense of visual images, graphic elements, and hypertextual connections. It involves the juxtaposition of texts that offer differing information and the critical thinking necessary to understand the perspectives involved in the production of these texts.

In similar fashion, writing is no longer simply putting pencil to paper; it is about designing multimodal texts by drawing on visual images, graphic elements, and other available resources in the process of making one's ideas visible. Once completed, our students can make their ideas visible to the entire world almost instantaneously through the Internet. This shift from the written word delivered through the printed page available in one classroom to the multimodal text distributed in digital formats around the world has changed everything about literacy education. The better we understand how to support students as they interact with web-based, digital, and multimodal resources to make their ideas visible and available, the better we will be positioned to be successful in the reading workshop 2.0 environment.

PART

READING
WORKSHOP 2.0
PROCESSES

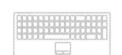

INTRODUCTION TO PART II

It is the kinds of texts children have access to and the kinds of interactions they experience around those texts that influence the kinds of readers they become.

—Margaret Meek, 1988

The reading workshop 2.0 framework is designed to provide teachers and students with digital and web-based resources and technologies for accessing and navigating, archiving and sharing, commenting and discussing, and interpreting and analyzing a variety of children's literature and multimodal texts. The resources described in this section provide new approaches for breaking away from traditional ways of accessing texts and responding to one's reading. Part II of this book introduces new web-based and digital tools for navigating, sharing, discussing, and analyzing the wide variety of texts readers encounter in the digital age.

Today's readers encounter children's literature, informational texts, magazines, newspapers, reference materials, and websites in all sorts of new formats and platforms. Consequently, the basic processes of accessing, navigating, sharing, discussing, and interpreting this material will need to evolve and expand. Although some of the basic processes associated with decoding, responding, and analyzing texts will remain the same, other processes will adapt to the changing nature of the texts being read. In Part II, I will share specific instructional approaches and lesson ideas that take into account how digital and web-based resources can be used to support the instructional components of the reading workshop 2.0 framework.

Although the processes of accessing, navigating, sharing, commenting, discussing, and analyzing might blend together or overlap in practice, I will present them separately here to provide instructional approaches for supporting these processes individually. In real life, as in classrooms, when does navigating text not entail some level of analysis, and when does commenting and sharing not lead to discussion? However, I feel there are enough distinctions among the four processes described here to warrant presenting them separately.

I will begin by briefly defining each of the four processes that will make up the second half of the book:

1. **Accessing and Navigating.** The ways in which readers access and navigate texts have changed drastically in the past ten years. Digital reading devices such as eReaders, tablets, laptop computers, and smartphones provide instant access to a wide variety of digitally based texts. Not only have the devices changed because of digital technologies, the

types of texts made available through these technologies and devices are different. Texts with hyperlinks, visual images, video segments, interactive components, and new formats and design features are commonplace, so new skills and strategies are needed to navigate and access them. As our reading lives move further along into the digital age, we must consider how the changes in what our students are reading now affect how we teach them new strategies for being successful readers.

2. Archiving and Sharing. As readers, we are able to archive and share what we read in new ways due to the resources available in digital environments. We used to have only physical bookshelves in our homes, libraries, schools, and offices; now we have digital bookshelves that house our electronic text collections, websites that keep track of the books we want to read, platforms for posting book reviews, and communication technologies for sending recommendations to our friends. Using digital highlighters, we can share what we think is important in a text with anyone around the world The ability to digitally archive our reading gives us a different perspective on ourselves as readers, and it allows others to peer into our reading lives and individual preferences and opinions.

3. Commenting and Discussing. Whether face-to-face or across the globe, we can now post comments about a favorite book and discuss these books with friends in real time (synchronous) or on our own schedule when we feel like adding our thoughts to a discussion board (asynchronous). We can make comments on paper sticky notes, or we can download one of the many apps available for commenting on digital texts. We can use video conferencing technologies like Skype or FaceTime to discuss ideas with other readers in our schools and around the globe via the Internet. In addition, there are many social media sites available for posting online reviews and participating in virtual book clubs. In today's web-based environments, we are able to discuss texts with different people in different ways, providing us with new perspectives and new opportunities to consider what others think about those texts.

4. Interpreting and Analyzing. There are numerous digital and web-based resources available for supporting the interpretation and analysis of the texts. Multimedia resources like Glogster and Wordle provide digital platforms for readers to create visual presentations in new and exciting formats. These technologies can also help us to interpret specific aspects of texts and images, take a closer look at sections of texts and images, and post analytical notes in the margins of texts and

can provide new avenues for closely reading and interrogating print-based and digital texts. This last section contains some of the most challenging, yet some of the most exciting, resources and instructional approaches to responding to and analyzing what we read.

At the end of each chapter in Part II, I have included three explicit lessons that show how teachers might demonstrate and support the reading processes discussed. Each explicit lesson is organized using the following headings:

- ▸▸ Rationale
- ▸▸ Objective
- ▸▸ Demonstration
- ▸▸ Resources
- ▸▸ Comments

I explain why each lesson is important, what my learning objective is, and how the actual lesson might proceed; I suggest resources for conducting each lesson and add some additional comments. An LCD projector, smart-board, or other method of projecting your computer or tablet's screen image is required for most of these explicit lessons. Students need to see how the teacher navigates the online and digital resources they are expected to explore and use before being asked to work independently. Teachers will support these lessons by thinking aloud about the choices they make when navigating these online resources. They will describe their learning objectives and offer play-by-play descriptions of what they are doing and thinking as they progress.

Digital technologies and web-based resources provide us with vast opportunities that were unavailable in the age of print-based texts only. However, many of the digital and web-based resources presented here will also provide support for sharing, discussing, and analyzing print-based texts as well. There is no need to clear classrooms of traditional print-based texts as we move into digital reading devices. Picture books, novels, informational texts, magazines, and textbooks can and should be accessed in whatever formats are available.

Each of the instructional approaches in Part II will require some knowledge of technology and/or digital environments. I know this may seem daunting to many teachers. I suggest that you download and access the suggested resources and play around with them to get a sense of how they work. Then, think about what they might do for you as a teacher. There are certainly different levels of knowledge required for working with these resources, but I have not recommended any resources that most teachers, if provided with a little time and a little patience, cannot use. For us to better serve the learners in our charge, we as teachers need to be learners first, trying out different resources, talking with other teachers about how they are using some of these technologies, and inviting our students to learn alongside us as we traverse this new terrain together.

The digital and web-based resources and instructional approaches described in Part II will support readers regardless of how they access the variety of texts or formats in which they are delivered. I share instructional ideas throughout this section for all types of texts, digital and print based. My purpose in this book is to provide instructional ideas that enhance the approaches I have suggested over the years with new technologies to support quality reading instruction in a digital environment.

CHAPTER FOUR

Accessing and Navigating Digital Texts

Young readers of digital texts must be encouraged to develop flexibility and persistence in the physical and mental navigation of evolving digital texts.

Kristin Javorsky and Guy Trainin, 2014

This chapter focuses on the strategies and practices associated with accessing and navigating digital and web-based texts. I will describe the various types of digital texts available and some of the characteristics of the reading devices that allow readers to access these texts. I will then provide an overview of the various software applications, or *apps*, that support reading and reading instruction. Then I will offer a set of criteria for selecting appropriate, high-quality digital texts and apps and suggest ways to support readers as they browse and access various texts. Finally, I will present several explicit lessons for accessing and navigating web-based and digital texts.

Digital Texts

Readers have been accessing and navigating print-based texts for centuries. Throughout history, from papyrus scrolls to the age of the printing press, print-based texts have been made available for people to read and archive. In today's world, access to print-based texts is primarily through libraries, schools, online retailers, brick-and-mortar bookstores or by borrowing them from friends and colleagues. It is easy for readers to share print-based texts with other readers or carry them around in their pockets and backpacks. And to read print-based texts you don't need a power source other than the sun, a lamp, or a flashlight. Readers can also give print-based books as gifts, lose them, keep them on bookshelves, display them as decorations, or pass them down to members of their families for generations. For centuries, what constituted a book has changed very little.

Everything has changed with the advent of digital technologies, the personal computer, and the Internet. By turning images and written language into digital bytes that can appear on a variety of electronic devices, including eReaders, smartphones, and laptop computers, we have changed the nature and possibilities of what we know as a book. In contrast to print-based texts, which have a set reading path, linear structures, fixed typography, and no need for an electronic connection, digital texts exhibit the following characteristics (see Figure 4.1).

Figure 4.1 Characteristics of Digital Texts

- Digital texts can be altered and personalized for different readers' preferences—for example, font size and backlighting.
- They feature hyperlinks that can take the reader from one page to another within the text or to other related online texts.
- Rather than having a table of contents, they feature sidebar navigational tools that allow readers to navigate to other pages from anywhere in a text.
- They include a variety of modes—photography, sound effects, music, video clips, diagrams, and interactive maps are some examples.
- Digital texts require power to work, which is usually provided by a rechargeable battery or electronic connection.
- They can be electronically copied, shared across the Internet, sent through email, or stored on remote servers ("in the cloud").
- They are searchable, allowing readers to look for particular words, phrases, or headings.
- They can be highlighted and bookmarked, and highlighted sections can be aggregated and viewed as a separate text.
- Like blogs, they can be created by individuals and easily posted on the Internet for others to read and respond.
- They can include reference materials such as dictionaries, maps, calendars, interviews, and reading guides.
- Digital texts and reading devices may offer readers *text-to-speech* capabilities, allowing the text to be read aloud to the reader.
- They can highlight the text being read aloud so readers can follow along with the story.
- Finally, they can be quickly translated into languages other than English.

In addition to the features listed in Figure 4.1, Dalton and Proctor (2008) suggested that digital texts have different levels of *interactivity*. They proposed that digital texts fall into one of the following four categories:

1. Linear text in digital form: novels on an eReader
2. Nonlinear text with hyperlinks: most web pages
3. Texts with integrated media: enhanced digital books
4. Text with response options: socially interactive features

Texts with differing levels of interactivity have different features and technologies associated with them. In general, *basic digital texts* look like print-based versions of texts, allowing readers to turn pages as they do with printed books and store them in digital libraries. These basic digital texts have been minimally adapted from their print-based counterparts. On the other hand, *enhanced digital texts* feature more extensive interactive features, including images, video clips, game modules, and links to social media. Enhanced digital texts are very different from the texts of our past and require new skills to access and navigate them.

Different types of digital texts can be accessed through a variety of digital reading devices and software applications, or *apps*. Some of these digital texts are downloadable, meaning you can store a digital file permanently on your own reading device or computer, while others are only available online or by inserting a CD or memory card into the reading device. Additionally, other texts are apps that feature interactive components and resources, and they can be accessed using a smartphone, tablet, or personal computer. Figure 4.2 contains an overview of the various types of digital texts available and an explanation or example for each. The list of digital texts is ranked in order of interactivity from least to most interactive.

Figure 4.2 Types of Digital Texts Available

- Printed texts scanned into digital files: electronically scanned pages from print-based books
- Audio books: audio recordings of print-based books that are read aloud
- Digital eBooks and textbooks: any books or textbooks in digital form for purchase or rent from a publisher or retailer such as Apple or Amazon
- Enhanced eBooks: books with interactive, multimedia features that are contained in the digital file requiring no Internet connection
- Interactive eBooks: books with interactive, multimedia features that require an Internet connection.

There are always limitations and possibilities associated with any new technologies. The same is true for digital and web-based texts. Digital texts can be easily stored and retrieved on a device or on a remote server ("in the cloud"). Readers can carry thousands of books on a single tablet or reading device for access anytime, anywhere, as long as they have power. Digital readers provide their own lighting source or backlighting that allows them to be read in dark places. Digital texts can be also be revised or updated as new information is discovered, making them more flexible and adaptable compared to print-based texts. Although many readers still love to read print-based books, the number of digital texts sold has increased every year since their introduction.

Audio Books

Audio books have been around longer than digital texts. As a beginning teacher I bought audio books on cassette tapes, which I enjoyed listening to when driving to and from school each day; this helped me keep up with the increasing number of children's novels being published. I also used audio books in my reading workshop, which became a listening center where students enjoyed hearing stories read aloud. These analog-based audio books featured narrators (often a celebrity or professional reader), sound effects, and accompanying background music. In my classroom, readers could follow along with a printed copy of the selected book or simply listen to an engaging rendition of one of their favorite stories.

Digitally based audio books no longer require readers to carry around about ten cassettes per book. Digital audio books can be accessed online or purchased individually from book retailers and downloaded onto various reading and audio devices for listening to in the car, on an airplane, or simply when walking around. Most digital reading devices can easily hold hundreds of digital audio books. Figure 4.3 lists some of the online resources available for audio books.

Audible.com, owned and operated by Amazon, is one of the largest suppliers of audio books and audio content. It charges a monthly fee and requires an Internet connection to download books. It charges about $15 per

---

Figure 4.3 Online Resources for Audio Books

- audiobooks.com: subscription fees for one book per month
- bookshare.org: free to qualified students
- bookshouldbefree.com: access to limited titles for free
- gutenberg.org: access to classic books read aloud for free
- techsupportalert.com/free-books-audio: clearinghouse for free audio books online

month to access books through Amazon. Digital audio books are also available through the iTunes bookstore, Google Play, Barnes & Noble, and other online retailers.

In addition to the audio book resources described here, a few years ago I developed a brochure for Random House to help teachers use audio books in their classroom. The brochure is available for free at: www.frankserafini.com/classroom-resources/audiobooks.pdf.

Digital Reading Devices

These are the devices most commonly used for accessing digital texts: dedicated digital reading devices such as the Amazon Kindle, Sony Reader, Kobo eReader, or Barnes & Noble Nook; tablets such as the Amazon Fire or Apple iPad; smartphones; and all types of applications available for reading eBooks on laptop and desktop computers. Although there are claims that more than 500 different digital reading devices are available, this list represents the most commonly used devices and those that will probably be around in the near future. Each of these devices translates digital code into a visual text and displays the text on some type of glass or plastic screen. Most of these devices have proprietary licenses that require digital texts to be purchased from their associated retailers. The good news is most eBook retailers—Google, Apple, and Amazon—offer free apps that can open a proprietary eBook across different devices. This means I can use the Kindle Reader app on my Apple computer, tablet, or smartphone to read books purchased through Amazon.

The first texts available for digital reading devices looked very similar to the traditional print-based texts, only they were displayed on an electronic screen. These early devices did not have many of the enhanced features available today and were limited to original print-based structures and formats. For the most part, these digital reading devices, like the first Kindle Readers from Amazon, featured black text on a white background and offered a limited selection of books. Since the arrival of the first digital reading device, the industry has exploded. Millions of digital books, both fiction and nonfiction, are now available for a variety of digital reading devices, as digital texts, apps, or audio books.

Different technologies allow readers to do different things with digital texts. Initially, readers could navigate digital texts on a reading device in much the same manner as a print-based book. Since the introduction of these early digital reading devices, additional features have been made available that allow readers to set their own reading preferences by altering the size and font of the text, highlight important sections, look up words in a built-in dictionary, write comments in pop-up text boxes and the margins, and share their comments, reviews, and recommendations with other readers across the Internet.

In addition to these developments in technology, how we interact with digital texts has changed as well. Readers now talk about being "a certain percentage through a book" because that's how their reading progress is measured on a digital device. They are able to sync where they are in a particular digital text across a variety of reading devices, like computers and smartphones. Readers can download books and store them in the cloud or on their personal reading devices. Readers can use virtual bookmarking tools, navigational buttons, and resources connected to the digital texts, like games and reference materials. Not only have the characteristics of the texts we read changed, the way we talk about them and the social practices associated with reading them have changed as well.

Navigating Digital Reading Devices

The *book-handling skills* necessary to access and navigate digital texts and reading devices need to be developed with readers as they interact with them (Javorsky and Trainin 2014). As the opening epigraph suggests, teachers need to be patient with young readers while they learn to be flexible and persistent working with these new features and technologies. It takes time to explore the various features of digital readers, exposure to how other readers use them, and opportunities to experiment with how to access and navigate texts on digital reading devices.

Unlike print-based texts, readers don't just simply locate the first page of a digital book, open it up, and start physically turning its pages. Instead, readers are required to know how to turn these devices on and ensure they are properly charged. They need to know how to access digital libraries, select a particular text to read, and navigate through the text once it has been identified. Readers also need to know how to sync digital texts across devices, access features like dictionaries and text-to-speech technologies, and highlight and comment on what they are reading.

Many digital reading devices offer navigational devices such as touch screens and tilt-technologies that foster navigation by pressing buttons or tilting the actual device itself. In addition to visual icons on the screen itself, many reading devices feature buttons and sliders located on the actual device that help in its operation. Digital texts may also feature sound effects, animations, reference materials, and background music that can be distracting. Readers need to know how to disable these features to avoid being distracted by them as they read.

Most digital reading devices allow readers to instantly return to the beginning of a story or access the table of contents from anywhere in the text. They also have a particular method for turning the pages of a text, for example, by swiping across the screen or hitting a navigational icon or button. In addition, most digital reading devices offer hyperlinks embedded in the text for connecting to internal and external resources, ways of highlighting sections of the text, and a text-to-speech, or read aloud, option. How these features work varies across reading devices and requires some time and experimentation to get comfortable with handling them. Although all digital reading devices come with some form of digital or print-based user manual, nothing can substitute for allowing young readers time to explore the features of their digital reading device.

When starting to read a text on a digital reading device, readers should begin by setting their preferences for sound volume and text size and then learn how to turn the pages. Using features such as commenting and highlighting can come after readers learn how to initially navigate through a digital text. Next, readers must decide whether to read it themselves or have visual or audio assistance. Finally, being able to sync or bookmark one's place in a text for returning to it later is crucial for keeping track of one's reading progress. After these basic features have been mastered, readers may begin to take advantage of any enhanced features offered on their reading device. With an Internet connection, readers can also access a variety of resources associated with a particular book, such as book reviews, recommendations, interviews, book trailers, and other related materials.

There are two very important aspects of digital reading devices that classroom teachers should be aware of. First, what one reads on a digital reading device can be made more private than carrying around a hardcover book. Struggling readers can carry home books that are appropriate for them to read without worrying what anyone else thinks about what they are reading. Second, many digital texts are generally much cheaper than their print-based counterparts. This is an important consideration as we try to build classroom libraries and provide access and opportunities for our students to find their way into reading.

In addition to all of the affordances associated with digital reading devices, there are some challenges and limitations associated with them as well. Most digital reading devices are heavier than paperback novels and may be more difficult for young readers to hold comfortably. In addition, digital readers require some form of power source and must be charged regularly. Also, the backlighting featured on some reading devices may cause excessive eyestrain. Finally, there are numerous features of digital texts that may distract readers from the text they choose to read. Some of these features take readers away from reading, inviting them to play video games or connect with other readers over the Internet. However, I believe the possibilities far outweigh the challenges, and digital texts seem to be growing in popularity with every generation of readers.

Apps

Apps, short for software *applications*, offer some of the most exciting advances in digital technologies and an untapped potential for supporting readers in the reading workshop 2.0. There are literally thousands and thousands of apps available through distributors like Apple, Amazon, and Google Play. Apps provide a wide range of resources for entertainment, education, business productivity, photography, social media, and communication.

Book apps fall somewhere between the children's literature market, where digital publishers are looking for works of literature to adapt, and the new digital formats and features associated with the gaming or entertainment industry (Turrion 2014). To be successful, the hybrid features of book apps require readers to have experience with the structures and formats of literature in addition to those of electronic media.

A quick tour through the iTunes or Google Play stores, as well as other online retailers, reveals an amazing variety of apps associated with reading and children's literature. There are so many apps available nowadays that trying to keep up with what is being offered is virtually impossible. The best way to get started is to read reviews online about the quality of various apps available. In addition, most publishers offer some form of free, or *lite*, versions of their apps with the opportunity to upgrade to full versions later. I suggest trying out the free versions of an app before upgrading to the full version whenever possible.

The iTunes website offers a wide variety of book apps organized into the following categories: comics and graphic novels, children's and teen literature, books based on TV and movies, fiction and literature, and nonfiction. There are numerous apps offered in each category; some are free, and others are priced from ninety-nine cents. After an extensive review of the apps that could be used to support readers in a reading workshop 2.0, I suggest teachers explore and consider the following six types of apps:

1. Apps for searching and purchasing digital texts

2. Apps for displaying and reading digital texts

3. Apps for aggregating web-based content

4. Apps that offer enhanced features of texts that are contained in the app itself

5. Apps that offer interactive features and connect texts to social media and other online resources

6. Apps for reading instruction and skill development

The apps listed in the six sections that follow are easily retrieved from the iTunes, Google Play, or Amazon websites or by searching the Internet with the name of the app provided here. Regardless of your preferred platform, these apps are capable of being used on a variety of tablets, smartphones, computers, and other reading devices. Along with a description of the features of each type of app, I have included a short explanation of how they might be used in the reading workshop 2.0.

Apps for Searching and Purchasing

Apps used for searching through available digital books, magazines, newspapers, and other digital content are usually free to download but sometimes require *in-app purchases* of content. These apps serve as platforms for reviewing and purchasing books, magazines, newspapers, and other digital content. These apps also allow readers to search through vast databases of digital content and read reviews and recommendations based on one's interests and purchasing histories.

Of course, Amazon.com provides one of the largest online databases of books for purchase, book reviews, and other associated content. Amazon and many online book retailers also offer apps that allow readers to search and purchase digital texts from their mobile devices. Some of my other favorite web-based booksellers that offer large collections of digital and print-based books, as well as online reviews and recommendations are Powells.com; barnesand-noble.com; bookweb.com (American Booksellers Association website); and bookfinder.com, which serves as a clearinghouse for other sites offering digital content. Some of these book retailers—Barnes & Noble, for example—offer apps that can be used on a mobile device to search their online databases. Powells Books even offers an app for navigating and searching for books in their brick-and-mortar bookstore in Portland, Oregon!

Three websites that offer extensive social media platforms as well as providing book-search capabilities are Goodreads.com, Librarything.com, and Shelfari.com (operated by Amazon). I have been a member of Goodreads.com for several years and have used this resource with my college students for posting book reviews and supporting discussion groups (more on these uses in later chapters). I prefer Goodreads.com because it provides a mobile app, free of charge for my smartphone and tablet, which allows me to quickly scan ISBN codes of any books and add them to my wish lists or reading lists on my Goodreads account. By searching Goodreads.com, you can instantly connect to your preferred online book retailers and purchase any books you find interesting. The other two sites also offer extensive cataloguing features and can connect readers to other readers in groups and discussion boards. In addition, LibraryThing offers a search engine for locating local brick and mortar bookstores.

The Zinio app, offered free on the Zinio.com website, promotes itself as the world's largest newsstand. The app allows readers to organize and retrieve copies of any newspapers, magazine, and other digital content to which they subscribe. Newsstand is an app from Apple that comes preloaded on their mobile devices and serves similar purposes. Both apps require subscriptions or in-app purchases to access most of the digital content. Some newspapers, however, provide some free content and offer digital access to their entire collection free of charge with a subscription to their print versions. In the past several years, I have chosen to have many of my magazine and newspaper subscriptions (*The New Yorker*, *New York Times*, *Outdoor Photographer*, *Arizona Highways*, and *MacWorld*) changed to digital access or a blend of print and digital access. I enjoy being able to carry numerous subscriptions and issues of these magazines and newspapers around on my tablet for reading when I travel.

Two of my favorite apps for accessing, searching, and purchasing digital texts are Kids Media and Book Finder. These two apps are available in the iTunes store, on Amazon.com, and through Google Play. The Kids Media app is an excellent resource for locating reviews about books, movies, apps, websites, video games, and other digital content. Book Finder is a search engine for locating free books online at websites such as iBookstore, Feedbooks, and Project Gutenberg. Reading reviews and recommendations offered on these websites and apps is an excellent way to help readers find appropriate and interesting things to read. Openlibrary.org also provides a large database of digital books that can be downloaded or borrowed for a specific length of time.

Along with well-known websites like Amazon.com and Goodreads.com and traditional resources like the *New York Times Book Review* and *Publishers Weekly*, the websites listed in Figure 4.4 are excellent online resources for reviews of books and digital content for children.

Apps for Reading

Some book apps include the complete text in the app itself, while others are simply platforms for downloading separate digital texts. The apps that require in-app purchases are usually offered for free but require the purchase of the

---

Figure 4.4 Online Resources for Reviewing Digital Books and Content

- Kirkus book reviews: kirkusreviews.com
- bookbrowse.com
- carolhurst.com
- eleanorsbooks.com
- bookhive.org
- The Horn Book: hbook.com
- justonemorebook.com
- International Digital Children's Library: en.childrenslibrary.org
- kidlitosphere.org
- storylineonline.net

actual digital texts. The apps described in this section serve as reading platforms for purchasing and downloading digital content. The most widely used apps for reading digital content are iBooks (Apple), Play Books (Google), and Kindle Reader (Amazon). In addition, many of these apps have creative counterparts; for example, iBooks Author from Apple allows students to create online and digital content as well as read it.

There are apps available that will read a digital text aloud for readers. Two apps that offer text-to-speech capability I have used are Talk to Me and Speak It. They cost about $2 and can be used with any PDF and other selected digital text formats. This capability provides support for struggling readers to work through tough sections of text or to hear how a particular word is pronounced.

Scribd is a relatively new online resource that provides a monthly subscription service for readers to access thousands of books. In much the same way that Netflix works for movies and Spotify works for music, scribd.com advertises that it has about half a million titles from over nine hundred publishers. With your monthly subscription (about $10) Scribd allows you to download an unlimited number of digital books and read them when you are offline as well as when you have an Internet connection. Scribd also allows writers to upload documents and make them available for sale to its eighty million subscribers. In addition, Amazon has recently launched Kindle Unlimited, a monthly subscription service for renting selected digital content (advertised as including over six hundred thousand books) from the Amazon database.

Apps are also available for purchasing and reading graphic novels and comics. *Marvel Comics* and *DC Comics* provide free apps for accessing their content, which in most cases requires additional purchases. ComiXology is an app that serves as a reading platform for a variety of comics, including the Bone series by Jeff Smith. Many of these platforms provide additional support for navigating graphic novels and comics by displaying one panel at a time and transitioning to the next panel automatically for the reader. In addition, these platforms offer many interactive features and connections to online resources and communities.

Other apps for reading provide free access to classic texts that are in the public domain to be retrieved and accessed on mobile devices and computers. Three apps for accessing free books online that I have used frequently are Shu-Book, MegaReader, and Stanza. These apps also provide features for readers to search and retrieve books provided free across the Internet. There are many apps that serve as platforms for accessing a variety of digital content on different types of digital reading devices, so readers have many choices.

Apps for Aggregating Online Content

There are apps that make your online reading life much easier. These apps aggregate content and resources from across the Internet and organize this information into self-selected or predetermined categories. In a sense, these *content aggregators* serve as online bookmarks, automatically gathering content into digital collections for sharing or reading at a later time. These content aggregators can help students keep track of the websites and online content they have been searching through for a research project or other educational project, and they allow students to share with their classmates the information they have located and organized. The apps listed here are some of the most popular ones for aggregating online content. Each of them is free to download, but they require users to create an online account to save and organize the content being bookmarked.

These content aggregators work in a variety of ways. First, buttons or icons can be downloaded and added to the navigation bar located on the top of most web browsers such as Safari, Firefox, Internet Explorer, and Chrome. After these extensions have been added to your web browser, you simply hit the application's icon in the navigation bar to add content that you find online to your collection. Second, you can download an app for your mobile device (tablet or smartphone) and add content to your account from these devices. Third, these aggregators can work on mobile devices and organize content to be synced back onto one's computer.

Two of my favorite content aggregators are Instapaper and Flipboard. Instapaper allows readers to archive, highlight, and browse online content and aggregate it into saved folders for sharing and reading. The web-based interface looks similar to a newspaper layout and is easy to navigate. Other aggregators that work similar to Instapaper are Delicious and Sqworl. Each has its own navigational icons and layout, but they work in essentially the same manner.

Flipboard works a bit differently than some of the other aggregators. You can link Flipboard to your Twitter and Facebook accounts, as well as subscribe to a variety of content choices offered by Flipboard. Your home page in Flipboard serves as a navigational space, allowing you to read content from any of your saved categories. Flipboard goes out to the Internet and gathers news reports, blogs, and other content based on your selected categories and aggregates the material for you so you don't have to search the web every day. I like Flipboard because it provides visual images and not just text boxes of the content being bookmarked.

There are aggregators that work specifically on RSS (Really Simple Syndication) *feeds*. Blogs and other web-based content providers generate RSS feeds, and these feeds are gathered and organized by an RSS feed aggregator. For example, you could use an RSS aggregator to follow my reading workshop blog. Rather than going to my blog website every day, you could use an RSS feed aggregator like RSS Notifier to subscribe to my blog. It would check my website every day and alert you when something new has been posted. There are lots of RSS aggregator apps and programs to choose from—Netvibe, Newsblur, Feedly, and Digg are a few examples. Other content aggregators work specifically on news content, such as Yahoo News, Pulse, and News 360.

Apps with Enhanced Features (self-contained)

Today there are literally thousands of book apps offering a range of enhanced features available for a variety of reading devices and platforms. These apps are downloaded from an app store or website and contain all of the information necessary for its operation in the digital file of the app itself. There are no required in-app purchases to make to use these types of apps.

Some of these enhanced book apps feature minimal enhancements, like the text being highlighted as a narrator reads aloud, music in the background, simple sound effects, small buttons to press that animate portions of the illustrations, or pop-up boxes that identify characters by name. Some examples of this type of book app are *The Tale of Peter Rabbit* (PopOut! Books), *The Cat in the Hat* and other books by Dr. Seuss (Ocean House Media), and *Alice in Wonderland* (Atomic Antelope). In many cases, *lite versions* of these book apps are offered free of charge to download but may require in-app purchases to access more stories or the full features of the book. A simple perusal of the Apple App Store, Amazon, or Google Play reveals hundreds of enhanced books.

One of my favorite enhanced book apps is *The Fantastic Flying Books of Mr. Morris Lessmore*, written by William Joyce and created by Moonbot Studios. This book actually began as an animated short film, which won an Academy Award before being made into a book app and subsequently a hardcover picture book. The animated film has no written narrative, only background music and sound effects to support the animation. The book app has narrative text that can be read by the reader, or it can be read aloud by a recorded voice as readers follow along with the highlighted text. The book app also offers enhanced elements that add to the story and illustrations.

Other favorite enhanced book apps are *Don't Let the Pigeon Run This App* by Mo Willems. This app features Willem's famous pigeon from his book series and allows readers to create and play back their own pigeon stories. *The Monster at the End of This Book* from Sesame Street is a wonderfully enhanced book that teaches young readers how to navigate the book and not be afraid of unknown things. The classic book *Animalia* by Graeme Base has been made into a book app by Base Factory and offers readers sound effects, close focusing, and gaming capabilities. These apps are available for around $5.

Most of the enhanced book apps support young readers by providing visual cues for teaching them how to swipe to turn pages, icons that signal which enhanced features are available, and highlighted text that enables them to follow along with the oral narrative. A detailed list of things to consider when selecting book apps is presented later in this chapter.

Apps with Interactive Features (online)

Book apps that incorporate interactive features require readers to be connected to the Internet to access these additional resources. For example, many publishers have created video games that connect to their stories and characters, offer clues in the text and online to follow to complete assignments and adventures associated with their books, and house online communities of readers that provide opportunities for discussions and sharing of ideas with other readers.

The first book I encountered years ago that offered online resources and interactive features was a novel called *Skeleton Creek* by Patrick Carman (2009). The book is separated into two parts: one character, Ryan, whose text is featured in journal form inside the print-based book; and another character, Sarah, whose narrative videos are offered on a website with links and passwords to the videos displayed in the printed text. There are now four books in the Skeleton Creek series. Video clips on Patrick Carman's website explain how the books were created and provide instructions for how to navigate these multimedia books. Other resources connected to these books are available on the website, including podcasts, author interviews, discussion boards, and study guides for teachers. Patrick Carman is also the author of The 39 Clues series published by Scholastic. Scholastic also offers multimedia, interactive apps for other book series, including Spirit Animals, Infinity Ring, and Tombquest. Each of these book series has an associated online community and affinity space for readers to interact with the books and other readers.

From classics like *The Wizard of Oz*, *The Adventures of Sherlock Holmes*, and *Alice in Wonderland* to Disney stories and contemporary children's literature, books are being created anew and provided in digital formats. Some apps retain similarities to print-based versions, while others are multimodal, multimedia ensembles that offer enhanced and interactive features. Some of these features may support the reader, but other features may only serve as distractions, taking the reader farther and farther away from the original text being offered. Teachers will need to preview these enhanced and interactive texts to determine their instructional potential.

Apps for Reading Instruction

I am most critical of some of the apps that purport to help struggling readers develop their reading abilities. Too often, these apps operate in the same manner as the print-based worksheets we moved away from years ago. Educational book publishers, including Penguin, McGraw-Hill, Houghton Mifflin, and Scholastic, offer apps for reading instruction, but my cursory review suggests they look more like basal instruction manuals than books children will want to read.

There are so many apps available for reading instruction that to even survey this landscape would require another book by itself. There are apps that connect to the Common Core Standards, that help support learning a foreign language, that provide vocabulary and phonics instruction, that provide quizzes and other reading assessments, and that teach the alphabet and basic print concepts. Reading Rainbow has an app that offers in-app purchases and includes a huge library of books and video field trips connected to its featured stories. However, teachers need to carefully review these resources and consider whether they may waste students' time by providing more entertainment than education. I will just say that building a diorama or completing a worksheet is a waste of time whether our students do it with a pencil and a shoebox or online.

Selecting High-Quality Book Apps

Deciding what constitutes a high-quality book app is similar to deciding what constitutes high-quality literature. In many ways these decisions are based on a wide range of factors; they are subjective and usually depend upon a reader's preferences, interests, and purposes. What makes a good book depends on the quality of the narrative, the writing itself, the art, and the book's design elements. It also depends on the reader.

In addition to the traditional criteria for selecting quality literature—award winners, publisher recommendations, and bestsellers as a few examples—the criteria for selecting quality book apps must take into account the technological and navigational aspects of the book app as well as the narrative itself. The list of questions presented in Figure 4.5, compiled and adapted from Yokota and Teale's (2014) and Johnson's (2014) published criteria, should be considered when selecting books in digital formats.

In addition to these questions, there are many online resources available for locating critical reviews of book apps available for reading and children's literature. I suggest that teachers spend time reading reviews before purchasing

---

Figure 4.5 Criteria for Selecting High-Quality Book Apps

1. Is the story appropriately presented in digital format? What features have been removed or changed from the original story?
2. Is the app easy to navigate?
3. Are the illustrations of high quality and well designed?
4. Are the sound effects, background music, and/or narrator's voice appropriate for the story?
5. Does the story provide features appropriate for the story?
6. Do the interactive features distract the reader from the story?
7. Is there any instructional potential in the features the app provides?
8. Do the features appropriately support beginning and young readers?
9. If available, are reference materials easily accessed?
10. What have reviewers said about the app? What do your students think about the app?

Figure 4.6 Online Reviews of Book Apps

- commonsensemedia.com (Kids Media app)
- appadvice.com
- kidsbookapp.com
- iTunes Store
- Google Play Store
- amazon.com
- kirkusreviews.com
- hbook.com
- digital-storytime.com

apps or recommending them for their students' use. Some of my favorite online resources for locating reviews of book apps are listed in Figure 4.6.

The final web-based resource that I feel teachers need to access and participate in is Twitter, a social media site that has emerged as one of the most expansive platforms, probably second only to Facebook. What makes Twitter so valuable is that teachers are one of its leading demographics. Teachers have been sharing resources through Twitter feeds for about five years or more. Following particular hashtags (#) that aggregate individual posts, or *tweets*, or individual Twitter sites (@), teachers can quickly explore a wide range of resources for educational purposes. My Twitter site is located at @doctorserafini. Every day I try to post resources for reading, children's literature, and literacy education. Other popular literacy educational hashtags are #edtech, #socialmedia, and #literacyeducation.

Digital reading devices and other technologies may engage readers initially, but what we do with this technology determines whether they continue to engage in the act of reading. If we fall back into the "old wine in new bottles" syndrome, enticed by the lure of new technologies but no actual changes in practice, it won't matter whether our dioramas are made out of cardboard or pixels. The focus has to remain on the impact of the experiences provided in the reading workshop 2.0 regardless of the platform or device from which the resources or lessons are derived. Goodreads.com is a resource for searching, accessing, and sharing digital content. The goal is not to get better at using Goodreads.com; rather, it is to get better at accessing and selecting quality things to read.

When working with novice readers, we need to balance our instruction of reading skills with instruction of technology skills. It doesn't help if readers can't find the text they want to read, or if readers can find what they want to read but can't read it. Both are important considerations in the reading workshop 2.0. We need to help young readers navigate their reading devices and online resources while helping them become more proficient readers.

Many lifelong readers tell me they still prefer print-based texts for their professional and personal reading. However, most of them also acknowledge they have purchased a digital reading device for some texts and reading situations. I hope that both of these ways of accessing texts and information continue to be made available in our classrooms, allowing readers to choose how they access and navigate what they read. Many of our students might still prefer print-based texts for certain reading situations, while others will prefer to read everything on their reading devices. We need to allow readers to choose not only what they read but how they access what they read and how it is delivered and displayed.

Explicit Lessons for Accessing and Navigating Digital Texts

The following lessons focus on accessing and navigating digital texts.

Lesson #1 Accessing Digital Texts

Rationale: Readers need to know how to access digital texts from a variety of websites and online resources. Understanding how texts are accessed, how much they cost, where free books are located, and how to download them onto reading devices is an important skill in the digital age.

Objective: Readers will be able to search and access a wide range of digital texts and download these texts onto their digital reading devices.

Demonstration: Teachers will navigate selected web resources that provide access to digital books and content. Using various online resources, the teacher will demonstrate how to locate and access a variety of digital texts. Part of this lesson will focus on how to create digital bookshelves to catalog one's reading choices.

Resources: Zinio.com, ComiXology.com, iTunes store, Amazon, Project Gutenberg, Book Finder, and other retailers of digital content.

Comments: There are many different online resources for accessing digital content. Teachers need to demonstrate an array of resources because each one may have different navigational features and paths. Be sure to offer demonstrations across platforms, texts, and devices.

Lesson #2 Supportive Browsing

Rationale: Readers need help selecting appropriate reading material, and many struggling readers do not know what is available for them to read.

Objective: Readers need to be able to browse libraries and databases to take advantage of book reviews, reader recommendations, comments, genre categories, and other information that will help them make appropriate selections.

Demonstration: The teacher will select several online resources and databases and show readers how to access reviews and recommendations, navigate the ways digital content is organized, and develop criteria for making appropriate reading selections.

Resources: Amazon.com, Goodreads.com, LibraryThing.com, Shelfari.com, and others.

Comments: Helping readers develop a set of criteria and an array of strategies for choosing what to read is an important lesson for early in the school year. Having a discussion about ways to make better selections with students and generating a list of ideas together has been a very positive learning experience in my classes. Possible criteria for making appropriate choices might include:

- Start with what you are comfortable with, such as reading books in a series or by the same author.
- Find books that are connected to ones you have read—same genre, setting, characters, or authors.
- Ask friends or search online for recommendations.
- Read comments and reviews.
- Browse covers, author blurbs, book blurbs, and advertisements.
- Read a few pages to determine whether the book is manageable.
- Consider the recommended reading level posted on the book.
- Ask the teacher or librarian for suggestions and support.
- Be willing to put a book back if it is too confusing.

Lesson #3 Navigating Digital Reading Devices

Rationale: Digital reading devices require readers to navigate digital texts using techniques that are different from reading and navigating print-based texts. Although some readers may have more exposure to digital reading devices, it is important to be sure all students are able to navigate and make use of the features associated with different reading devices.

Objective: Readers will learn how to navigate different digital reading devices and be able to set preferences for their devices, access a range of texts, take advantage of basic search features, use scrolling and scanning techniques, and understand how to sync what has been read across digital devices.

Demonstration: Teachers need to find ways to project a mobile device or computer interface so that they can show readers how to navigate various devices. This lesson focuses on five strategies: (1) set, (2) select, (3) scan, (4) search, and (5) sync.

Teachers should be able to demonstrate to students how to:

1. Set preferences: Adjust backlighting, font size, narration, and sound effects.

2. Select what to read: Return to the digital library from a particular text location, and select other texts to read.

3. Scan the device: Make use of the scrolling icons, page-turning options, table of contents and other guides, and reference materials such as dictionaries.

4. Search the text: Use the search feature to search for particular phrases, words, and headings in the text.

5. Sync with other devices: Use online connections to sync to the farthest point read across reading devices.

Resources: Online manuals available for different devices, video clips offered by retailers about how to navigate their reading devices, and tutorials included on the device itself.

Comments: As teachers and readers explore the features of their digital reading devices, a discussion concerning which features support reading and which features distract the reader or takes the reader away from the text is worthwhile.

Hyperlinks are sometimes inserted into digital texts to connect to internal resources on the reading device or external resources on the Internet. Although these links can be very useful at times, they can also distract readers by offering them superficial and irrelevant information. Readers need to be able to recognize when their attention has been taken away from the task at hand.

CHAPTER FIVE

Archiving and Sharing
Our Reading Lives

We possess the books we read, animating the waiting still-
ness of their language, but they possess us also, filling us with
thoughts and observations, asking us to make them part of
ourselves.

—David L. Ulin, 2010

Developing our students' identities as readers is as important as developing
their navigating and decoding skills. One way to help students see themselves
as readers is by documenting their reading lives and sharing this information with other readers. As lifelong readers, we keep track of those books we
possess and cherish; we look at our reading history patterns, which might not
be noticed as we go about our daily lives; and we find traces of ourselves among
the stacks of books we collect. Online resources can be used to archive one's
reading activities, interests, and preferred genres, and they can help us take a
closer look at our reading lives and histories. This chapter offers teachers several
web-based and digital resources designed to help children keep track of their
reading, generate book lists, share their reading preferences, post book reviews,
read book recommendations, and organize a collection of digital and print-
based books.

Print-based student portfolios have been used, misused, discarded, and rein-
troduced by many schools and districts over the past thirty years. Keeping track
of students' work, storing these collections, evaluating them, and using them
to drive instruction has had its ups and downs in literacy education. Online

and digital portfolios have been used with similar outcomes in elementary, high school, and college settings. In some ways, several of the resources I will be describing in this chapter are akin to online and digital portfolios—they are collections of books read, comments made, reviews read and created, and wish lists generated by individual readers. By archiving our students' reading lives we learn more about them as readers and are able to use this information to drive our instructional decisions and lessons.

The primary purpose of archiving one's reading life is to come to know oneself as a reader. I am not advocating the formal evaluation of one's reading life by counting the number of books read or using a rubric to evaluate book reviews that have been written and posted. Developing one's identity as a reader is an end in itself. Archiving what our students do as readers doesn't necessarily need to be graded to have a positive effect on their reading lives. Through participation in a community of readers, both in our classrooms and in online environments, our students come to see themselves as more capable readers.

Web-Based and Digital Resources for Archiving

There are many ways to organize our books. In our homes and offices we arrange them on bookshelves, display them on coffee tables, keep them close by on our nightstands, and store them on book racks. These displays reflect our histories as readers. Anyone who visits us can wander around and browse the artifacts of our reading lives. For centuries the great libraries of the world have created elaborate coding systems for organizing and retrieving print-based books and documents. With the emergence of digital books and documents, the ways we organize our books and how we display our reading histories is rapidly changing.

Digital Bookshelves and Lists

I keep many of my digital books stored on my iPad now, so someone would have to ask to borrow my reading device to browse through the books I am reading or have read, books that I used to display on the shelves of my home and office. A quick look at my Kindle Reader and iBooks apps reveals the variety of books and documents I have stored on my device or in the cloud for access later. If our students are beginning to read digital books on various devices, they have already begun to amass a collection that could be shared with other interested readers.

I love looking through people's bookshelves, both in paper and digital formats, to see their book collections. It gives me insight into their interests, personalities, and experiences. The same goes for the readers in my classroom. I don't want the sharing of digital bookshelves or their online *wish lists* to turn into a contest to see who has read the most or who has gathered the most titles. Rather, I would prefer that the sharing of these collections helps us get to know one another—to support our development as readers, foster our sense of community, and provide opportunities to talk about various strategies for selecting books.

Creating a list of favorite books and posting it online for other readers to view is another way of sharing your reading life. Amazon offers a service on its website, Listmania, that allows readers to create a list of up to forty books organized in a variety of ways and then share these lists with other readers. There are thousands of lists created by readers and archived on the Amazon website. Anyone with an Amazon account can also create a series of *wish lists* by organizing books to be read or purchased into specific categories. The wish lists I have generated on the site are organized into the following categories: professional books, picture books, children's novels, novels, photography books, and nonfiction titles. I can keep my wish lists private, or I can make them available to particular groups or the general public.

Readers can also find many booklists already created and posted online by individuals and various organizations. The American Library Association (ala.org) and the International Reading Association (reading.org) each post lists of award-winning books, children's choices, teachers' choices, and other excellent booklists for students and teachers to browse. In addition to Amazon and Goodreads, booklistonline.com offers many lists for readers and connections to many other lists of books organized by genre, theme, and content area. Booklists and digital bookshelves offer readers a way of organizing, archiving, and sharing their reading lives and, by looking at other readers' shelves and booklists, ways to find new books and get to know other readers.

Library Programs and Apps

Probably my favorite app for archiving my complete collection of children's and young adult literature is Delicious Library 3. The software program and the associated mobile app allow me to scan the ISBN codes of my books (or anything else with an IBSN code—DVDs, CDs, etc.) and organize them into categories or digital bookshelves by various genres or specific purposes. I now have over six thousand books scanned into my collection on this program. I can organize my digital bookshelves into a variety of categories and easily generate booklists from these collections to share with my students and fellow teachers.

Delicious Library 3 can also keep track of books when I lend them to friends and colleagues. Classroom teachers could easily use this program for organizing and maintaining their classroom libraries. Teachers can also connect their Delicious libraries to other teachers' libraries for sharing resources and lending books. At the time of writing this book, the program costs $25 and comes with a free mobile app you can download for scanning books from your smartphone or tablet.

I use my smartphone as a *mobile scanner* to scan the ISBN codes and upload the information over a Wi-Fi or Bluetooth network directly to my computer. Of course, the program also makes recommendations of books for readers to consider and links directly to online bookstores for purchasing new books.

The Delicious Library 3 program can also be used to create digital bookshelves for every student in the classroom. Teachers can create a separate shelf for each student, and students can simply scan the ISBN codes of the books they have read onto their digital bookshelves. This program also has interesting compilation and graphing capabilities that can visually represent the books one has read and archived and organize them into visual representations by genre or author. This is a wonderful program that teachers can use in their classrooms without needing lots of technical knowledge and upfront learning time. You can find more information at delicious-monster.com.

Two other web-based programs that offer similar capabilities are Classroom Organizer from BookSource and Readerware. Classroom Organizer allows teachers to generate library collections in much the same way as Delicious Library 3, but this website houses the lists online rather than on one's computer. Students can create collections and check out books from the program. Classroom Organizer also generates recommendations for purchasing books based on what one has in their collection and provides reports on students' reading activities. The Classroom Organizer program is free of charge but requires readers to create an account at classroom.booksource.com. One needs to remember that this is a commercial book retailer and one of its primary goals is to get you to buy books from Booksource. Many free and lite versions of commercial programs and apps come with advertising displays that can usually be removed by upgrading to their premier accounts.

Readerware is another library program that organizes your collection of books with an ISBN code. This program comes with a handheld wand for scanning the codes on books, making it possible for even young readers to scan the books they are reading and create their individual *digital reading logs*. These library programs offer numerous resources for organizing one's library, but with a little imagination they can be used to keep track of students' reading and other ways of archiving students' reading lives. As readers archive more and more books read on these library programs, the recommendations offered to individual readers become more targeted toward their reading histories.

Web-Based and Digital Resources for Reviewing and Recommending

The resources listed in this section can be used to read and post book reviews and recommendations. They can also be used to generate recommendations for readers based on what they have already read and archived on their digital bookshelves, wish lists, or classroom libraries. Some of these resources have been mentioned previously and some will be presented again in a later chapter because they offer a broad range of capabilities beyond simply archiving and sharing reviews and recommendations.

Several of these resources require one to be a bit more *tech savvy* than those offered in Chapter 4. Extensive experience with photography-editing software and audio-video recording devices is not necessary for working with the resources in this section, but it certainly would be helpful. For example, creating digital book trailers will require a digital or web camera that records video and a microphone for audio, but these are often built into recent computers or are easily obtained from an electronics or computer store. Most of the technologies necessary for using the resources mentioned in the next sections are contained on the websites themselves, and all of them have detailed instructions and tutorials for their use.

Social Media for Readers

In the previous chapter I mentioned using Twitter to post and share resources, reviews, and recommendations; I have been sending out (*tweeting*) educational resources to my followers on Twitter for a couple of years. And, of course, students could always post book reviews on Facebook for their friends to see. However, the social media sites listed throughout this chapter were specifically designed for readers and authors to share resources with other readers, authors, and, of course, publishers and booksellers. I mentioned previously how Goodreads.com could be used to archive a collection of all the books one has read or all the books in a classroom library collection. But that just skims the surface of the potential of this website and others like it.

In addition to reviews posted on Amazon and the iTunes bookstore, Goodreads.com, LibraryThing.com, and Shelfari.com archive millions of book reviews posted by adults and young readers. There are hundreds of pages of reviews of most of the popular children's books and plenty of reviews for lesser-known books. These sites also have discussion boards where members can get involved in online discussions of their favorite stories with readers from around the world (more about online discussions in the next chapter).

Websites like Shelfari, Goodreads, and LibraryThing are social media sites that cater especially to readers. In the same way that Facebook and MySpace are used for connecting and sharing with friends about one's social life, these sites that focus on reading are places for readers to create an online identity, post and organize the books they have read, read and write book reviews, and get recommendations for new things to read. After setting up an account and adding books to one's collection, these social media sites generate recommendations based on what one has gathered on their bookshelves. In addition to the recommendations generated through my Amazon account, Goodreads.com is one of my favorite resources for finding new books to read because the recommendations they offer are targeted directly at me based on my reading history. Many times, the recommendations I am offered on Goodreads.com are books I might not have ever found on my own.

In addition, these sites encourage readers to join discussion groups, make online friends (as in to *friend* someone) to see what others have been reading, take quizzes or participate in trivia contests, and join in other online activities within a community of readers. It takes just a few minutes to set up a free account and start posting books; however, there is a lot to navigate on these sites beyond simply posting books, so it will take time to explore all the features available. Each of the three sites listed in this section offers similar resources and interfaces; I recommend that you choose one and explore the resources it offers and then imagine new ways these online resources can be used in your classroom.

I have been using Goodreads with my college students for over five years. Throughout the semester, I require my students to write numerous book reviews based on what they have selected to read each week. I also require them to friend at least three people in the class and respond to their friends' reviews and posts each week. In many ways Goodreads has taken the place of the traditional reading response journals I made students complete for years. This program has extended the audience for my students' responses and book reviews beyond myself to other classmates and the reading world beyond our classroom walls. Writing a book review is an important skill for young readers and writers to develop. One of the explicit lessons later in this chapter focuses on how to write a quality book review.

Blogs

Another way for students to share what they have been reading and make recommendations for other readers is by creating and maintaining a *weblog* or *blog*. A blog is a chronologically ordered journal of short entries posted online for other readers to read and respond. Some of the more popular and long-standing websites for creating and hosting blogs are Blogger.com, Tumblr.com, and Wordpress.org. Two other blogging sites that focus on educational blogs are edublogs.com and campuspress.com. These blogging sites offer numerous templates from which to choose and house your blog for free when you sign up for an account. In addition, these blogging sites allow you to post text, images, video clips, links to other online resources, quotes, and audio files to your site. I have created blogs using several of these web-based software programs; I continue my blog for reading educators at thereadingworkshop.blogspot.com and my blog for nature photographers at backcountryimages.tumblr.com. Each of the three major blogging sites (Tumblr, Blogger, and Wordpress) also offer mobile apps that connect to one's account and allows you to post to your blog from your smartphone or tablet.

On my reading workshop blog (thereadingworkshop.blogspot.com), I have been posting "Picturebook of the Day" resources for the past year to share some of my favorite picture books with fellow educators. For each blog entry, I post an image of the cover of the book and offer a short synopsis and review of the selected picture books. On my reading workshop blog site, I also post excerpts from my professional writing (see Figure 5.1). I have included teaching tips, lists of resources for literacy educators, and lesson ideas. Finding blogs that offer information you and your students are interested in and following along with someone's posts can be very educational and entertaining.

Figure 5.1 Reading Workshop Blog

In our classrooms, students can be shown how to search through various blogging sites and find blogs that offer resources about books, authors, or genres that interest them. Searching through various blog sites with the keywords *children's literature* or *children's book reviews* reveals hundreds of blogs dedicated to talking about books for young readers. Using one of the aggregators described in the last chapter, students can automatically keep track of all the reviews and recommendations posted on their favorite blog sites.

In addition to having students read other peoples' blogs, we could also invite students to develop their own blogs and have classmates follow their book reviews. It is very easy to get a student blog up and running quickly using the software and templates provided on the most common blogging websites. Writing blogs can be taught within a unit of study focusing on blogs as a genre of writing. Hicks (2009) and Kist (2010) offer numerous ideas about how to get student-generated blogs up and running and how to maintain them over time.

Blogs are a form of social media that allow readers and writers to connect across time and location and share their ideas, interests, and opinions with other readers and writers. Whether we have our students follow someone else's blog or create one of their own, these online resources are excellent platforms for archiving and sharing book lists, reviews, and recommendations. Additional websites for hosting blogs for students are:

▸▸ epals.com
▸▸ classblogmeister.com
▸▸ socialmediaclassroom.com.

Video Booktalks and Book Trailers

There is a wide range of digital booktalks or book trailers available online. Many children's publishers, like Scholastic.com, have archived booktalks, including those done by authors and illustrators themselves. Booktalks can also be found on YouTube, though it takes some searching to find high-quality ones. Other websites are dedicated specifically to posting booktalks and trailers. Some websites dedicated to digital booktalks and trailers are:

▸▸ digitalbooktalks.net
▸▸ booktrailersforreaders.com
▸▸ bookwink.com
▸▸ schooltube.com

The quality of these booktalks and trailers can range from basic audio or audio-video recordings of a child talking about his or her favorite books to elaborate, professionally produced reviews of classic, contemporary, and newly released books. Readers can browse through the recommendations provided in audio-visual formats and use these resources to make more informed selections for their own readings.

In addition to searching through archived booktalks and book trailers to find reviews and recommendations, some of these websites offer students the opportunity to create and post their own video booktalks and trailers. Digitalbooktalks.net requires anyone wanting to post a digital booktalk to register on the site and submit their files for review before they can be posted. Book-trailersforreaders.com has a large selection of professionally made and student-generated book trailers and provides a link to the Sunshine State Young Readers Award books. This site also provides directions and resources you can download about how to make your own book trailers. Schooltube.com is a searchable database of videos produced by teachers and students on a variety of educational topics. Searching this database with the keywords *booktalks* or *book trailers* reveals hundreds of videos based on different books across grade levels. Some of the links to these videos work well, and others have been problems, so be patient searching these databases.

Although it may take a bit more knowledge of digital technologies and access to more audio-visual equipment, teachers can help students create their own book trailers and audio-video booktalks to post on their classroom website or share with other readers through the websites listed here. For me, the challenge in conducting book projects like these is making sure they don't end up being the equivalent of *digital dioramas*. Some of these projects take up so much time, time that readers could have spent actually reading. If you are comfortable with audio-visual recording technologies, then it may be possible to create digital booktalks in less time than it takes to read the book. More specifics about creating digital booktalks or trailers will be provided in a lesson at the end of this chapter.

Other Web-Based Resources

In addition to the resources described elsewhere in this chapter, I would be remiss if I didn't call your attention to the resources I provide free of charge on my website, frankserafini.com. Here you'll find links to all of my professional and children's writings, podcasts, blogs, and teaching resources. I have been generating booklists for years that are organized by genre, theme, author, illustrator, and content area. I try to update these booklists on a regular basis. I hope you find these resources valuable.

In addition to my website, Figure 5.2 lists several other websites that are excellent resources for locating booklists, book reviews, and book recommendations.

Keeping track of what our students read, making recommendations for fellow readers, and critically thinking about the quality of what one reads are all practices associated with a community of readers. These things are not just school-based projects; rather, they are social practices in which readers participate in the world outside of school.

Many of my college students have continued to add to their Goodreads accounts long after our semester together has ended. They have found a

---

Figure 5.2 Additional Web-Based Resources

- Online Podcasts About Books—justonemorebook.com
- Children's Literature Database—clcd.com
- Children's Book Reviews—thechildrensbookreview.com
- Kids Online Resources—kidsolr.com
- Canadian Children's Book Centre—bookcentre.ca
- Reading Is Fundamental—rif.org
- Book Reviews and Awards—readersfavorite.com
- Jon Scieszka's Website for Boy Readers—guysread.com
- Teen Book Review Network—teenreads.com
- Picturebook Reviews—picturebookmonth.com

---

community of readers with which to share their reading lives and identities and real purpose in engaging on this social media platform. This is a testimonial to the power of these social media platforms. I check updates on my own account to see what new books are being released and have found that the book reviews posted help me navigate the extensive number of books for children and young adults being published every year. Like my students, I too need high-quality reviews and targeted recommendations to become a more successful reader in the digital age.

Explicit Lessons for Archiving and Sharing One's Reading Life

The following lessons focus on resources and demonstrations for archiving and sharing one's reading life and reviewing and recommending books to other readers.

Lesson #1 Creating and Sharing Digital Libraries

Rationale: By keeping track of the books our students read we can help them develop a sense of identity as readers, find out what kinds of books they prefer, and help them share their reading lives with other readers.

Objective: Readers will learn how to scan books using a smartphone or enter them manually on a website or computer program that archives and organizes their reading histories for reviewing and sharing.

Demonstration: Depending on the program selected, teachers will demonstrate how to enter information into each reader's individual account or digital bookshelf. Teachers will need to first create a Goodreads.com or other social media site account, or set up their Delicious Library 3 program, to be able to demonstrate how to do this. It is important to feel comfortable with these various technologies before demonstrating them to students.

Resources: Goodreads.com, Shelfari.com, LibraryThing.com, Delicious Library 3, Classroom Organizer, or Readerware.

Comments: Buying a computer program for classroom use ensures that students' bookshelves remain private. Goodreads.com and other social media sites make readers' lives more public, although there are ways to limit access to students' accounts on these sites. Teachers need to explain about privacy settings to keep these archived collections private and their students protected.

Lesson #2 Writing Book Reviews

Rationale: Readers need to know what constitutes a well-written book review before they attempt to write one by themselves. To do this, students need to be exposed to a variety of book reviews, explore the style and characteristics of book reviews, and experiment with different types of them before posting their own for other readers to read.

Objective: Readers will be able to gather information about a particular book, draft and revise a book review, and post it online for other readers to read.

Demonstration: Teachers should begin by sharing numerous book reviews of varying quality with students. Using these examples, the class might create a chart of the characteristics of a high-quality book review. Figure 5.3 contains some suggestions for writing such a book review. Once readers have drafted, revised, and shared their book reviews, teachers will need to demonstrate how to post them on a website or classroom database.

Resources: Amazon, iTunes, Goodreads, Shelfari, and LibraryThing all have sections for reading and templates for posting book reviews. In addition, the following sites have numerous examples of student-created book reviews: readingrants.org, spaghettibookclub.org, and teenreads.com.

Comments: Discussing book reviews as a genre with specific conventions and craft elements brings a much-needed perspective to the teaching of this genre. Think about teaching the book review as you would any other genre, such as a personal narrative or poetry. Exposing students to a wide variety of book reviews, analyzing selected reviews for craft elements, and experimenting with different ways to create reviews are important steps in learning a new genre.

Book reviews are different from book reports only if they are posted somewhere for others to read and used by students to make appropriate

---

Figure 5.3 Suggestions for Writing a High-Quality Book Review

Parts of a Book Review

1. Summary of the story, including
    a. A two- to three-sentence summary of the story
    b. Design elements (picture books): borders, fonts, illustrations, etc.
    c. Narrative elements: plot, characters, setting, themes, etc.
2. Overall impression and a rating
3. Recommendations for other books readers might like

Suggestions for Writing

- Write a brief summary, no longer than two paragraphs, of the book. Usually a summary will build up to the main event and leave off before revealing any spoilers. Try to mention the name of the author and the book title in the first paragraph.
- Think about what genre the book might fit into. Is the book a mystery, a work of historical fiction, realistic fiction?
- If possible, use one paragraph for each point you want to make about the book. It's a good way to organize your writing and emphasize the importance of a particular point.
- Discuss possible themes of the book in your review.
- Make sure your review explains how you feel about the book and why, not just what the book is about. A good review should express the reviewer's opinion.
- Never be mean in a review. Remember that the author's heart and soul, and lots of time, were put into this piece of work. If you did not like something in the book, be constructive. Do not just say you hated it; say what you did not like in a constructive manner. Possibly talk about what you like or dislike about the author's craft and style.

---

choices for their selections. If the teacher is the sole audience for student-generated book reviews, they are no different than traditional book reports.

Lesson #3 Producing Video Booktalks and Book Trailers

Rationale: Creating video booktalks or book trailers is a more complex way to spur readers' interest in sharing the books they have read and make recommendations for other readers. Video booktalks can be as simple as having a student stand in front of a video-recording device and talk about his or her favorite books or as complex as creating multimedia book trailers using enhanced software programs and apps.

Objective: Readers will work with available software and computer equipment to create simple video booktalks or more elaborate book trailers.

Demonstration: Teachers will need to find examples of various levels of complexity of video booktalks and trailers to show students. They will also need to locate and explore software programs and recording equipment to support students as they work to create these multimedia projects. Finally, teachers will need to decide where and how these video files will be shared—online through a sponsored website like those mentioned previously, on the classroom website, or on classroom-based computers. Figure 5.4 lists steps to consider as teachers begin to work with students to produce these video projects.

Resources: Digital cameras with video capabilities, a video camera, or a computer with a camera and video-recording software; images of book covers from the actual books or found online; storyboard templates.

Comments: The level of expertise that teachers and students have in using digital recording software and equipment will dictate how complex these projects become. It is important to keep in mind that the goal of these projects is to get students to share what they have read, think critically about the books they select and read, and learn how to use various technologies to create and share these projects. Don't let the technology become the focus, especially as the projects become more complex.

Figure 5.4 Steps for Creating Digital Booktalks or Book Trailers

1. Choose a book that you have read and want to review and recommend.
2. Find examples of booktalks and trailers that are like the one you want to make. Find a mentor booktalk to use as inspiration!
3. Decide whether this will be a video of you talking about the book and holding it up, such as an oral book review, or a multimedia presentation using Prezi or PowerPoint with a voiceover.
4. Figure out what software and equipment you will need for the project.
5. Decide on sound effects, background music, and other enhancements if desired.
6. Start to draft the text of the booktalk. Remember that writing an oral booktalk to be recorded is different from a written book review.
7. Find digital images or video clips of high enough resolution to use in your trailer.
8. Use a storyboard to outline the structure of the digital trailer or booktalk.
9. Use recording or presentation software to create video booktalks or trailers.
10. Share booktalks and trailers with other students and the teacher for feedback.
11. Post video booktalks and trailers online for other readers to watch.

CHAPTER

Commenting on and Discussing Digital Texts

Talking well about books is a high-value activity in itself. But talking well about books is also the best rehearsal there is for talking well about other things. So in helping children to talk about their reading, we help them to be articulate about the rest of their lives.

—Aidan Chambers, 1996

This chapter includes two closely associated yet essentially different aspects of reading: commenting and discussing. The first, *commenting*, is primarily an individual, private act, and the second, *discussing*, is always a social one. Of course, comments can always be made public, but commenting begins with a single reader responding to what has been read and *marking up* a text in various ways either as one reads along or after finishing a book. Comments can be single words placed in the margins of a book that connect to some section or particular phrase, sometimes referred to as *marginalia*, or they can be longer, more formal pieces of writing such as critical essays or book reviews.

Discussions can be quite informal, where one reader simply tells another reader what they like or don't like about a book. Or, they can be more elaborate, where a group of readers gathers each month to talk about selected books. For the purposes of this chapter, the discussions I talk about and attempt to get teachers to facilitate are more extensive and detailed than a simple passing remark or unsupported judgment. In addition, discussions can take place in-person or online in real time (*synchronous*) or at different times and from different locations (*asynchronous*) by adding comments to an online discussion board either in writing or through a voice recording. Comments can be used as fodder for one's discussions, but it is the dialogic nature of social the interactions surrounding a text that provides the basis for the discussions I advocate.

In this chapter I will offer some thoughts on why we as readers code, comment on, and mark up texts ourselves, and why we might want our readers to do so as well. Next I will describe several web-based and digital resources for readers to mark up (code) or place comments on texts, particularly resources for doing this on a digital reading device. Finally, I will present various platforms and resources available to support readers when discussing books in real time (synchronous) with other readers and for readers to post comments on discussion boards, wikis, or other web-based platforms (asynchronous).

Some Thoughts About Coding and Commenting on Texts

As a reader, I have marked up texts in a variety of ways for many years. For example, I am an avid highlighter when I read, especially when I read professional books and journal articles about educational topics. I highlight sections of these texts with a bright yellow marker to help me identify and recall important ideas when I revisit these resources. I also write comments in the margins of my books, journal articles, newspapers, magazines, and other texts to remind me of my initial thoughts when I read them again. Through my years of teaching at the university, some of the copies of journal articles I have shared in my college classes have included my comments, or *marginalia*, and many students have seemed interested in what I commented upon when they read these articles for themselves. In the margins of texts I may write questions, single words, short comments on things I notice, connections to other texts, and analytical notes. However, because students in my elementary classrooms usually don't own the books we read in class, I do not allow them the same privileges I afford myself in regard to marking up or highlighting texts—that is, until we were provided access to digital texts!

For the past twenty-five years, in my classrooms at the elementary and college levels, I have been requiring readers to *code*, or mark up, texts they are reading as a way of preparing for literature discussions and sharing reading-comprehension strategies. I have accomplished this through the extensive use of paper sticky notes. I have purchased thousands of packs of sticky notes and have asked students to place them on sections of texts they feel are worth remembering or sharing. I also ask my students to write a word or two (code) on these notes as a reminder about what was important on that page. Because the books in my classrooms will be read by other students, the codes are placed on temporary sticky notes that can be removed sometime after the readings and discussions are completed.

After students finish reading a book and prepare for a literature discussion group, I have them review their sticky notes and make some notes about any patterns they have noticed about their reading of the text. After discussions are completed, I have students remove their notes and organize them with other readers into categories (see Figure 6.1). By reviewing the various categories that different readers created, students get some insight into how they read a particular book in addition to reviewing their initial reactions to the book on the individual sticky notes.

Figure 6.1 Multiple Coders

Nowadays, digital reading devices, apps, and computer programs not only allow readers to mark up texts in ways that are temporary and removable, they also allow readers to quickly aggregate their comments and share them with other readers around the world. In a Web 2.0 environment, what was once primarily an individual process of coding print-based texts can now be seen as a social process whereby readers share ideas and comment upon one another's codes and interpretations.

Before discussing the various devices and apps that provide platforms for creating and attaching comments, we need to think about *why* we want students to do this before teaching them *how* to do it. For many years my students in both elementary and college classes have asked me what to put on their sticky notes, how many stickies are required for each book, and what they are expected to do with them when they are finished reading. These are all logical questions, but they also reveal that students were not using the sticky notes for their own purposes; instead, they were simply following directions to complete an assignment.

As a reader, I don't comment on texts or write in margins to complete an assignment. Rather, I highlight or code texts, write comments, and review these codes and comments to help me make sense of and analyze the texts I read. Until our students understand the purposes behind these coding and commenting practices, they will simply complete the assignments we require of them and fill their books with useless sticky notes.

Larson (2010) studied the types of comments young readers generated using the commenting features on digital devices as they independently read fictional stories. By closely examining the comments made on the digital readers (Kindles) by second graders, Larson proposed five categories of readers' responses:

1. Retellings and personal commentaries
2. Meaning-making comments—connections and character identification
3. Asking questions
4. Answering questions in the text
5. Responding to text features

When provided with a digital reading device that supports highlighting and commenting, the young readers in this study did many of the same things with the digital devices they have done with traditional, print-based texts. Simply having students make comments on their digital reading devices does not take advantage of the resources found in a Web 2.0 environment. Readers are able to share comments and ideas online with other readers and see what aspects of texts have been commented on. This is the potential of Web 2.0 resources that we want to take advantage of in the reading workshop 2.0 environment. More about these features will be described shortly in this chapter.

Coding texts is simply a form of calling attention to particular elements in a text and commenting upon these elements. I have asked students to code texts to prepare for their literature discussions, suggesting that they place sticky notes on sections of the text they wanted to share or revisit and also include a word or short phrase to indicate why the sticky note was placed there. This process of coding texts is similar to the coding procedures researchers employ when conducting qualitative research projects. For example, when conducting an analysis of the data for one of my research studies, I begin by reading through the field notes, interviews, and transcripts and then code these texts with words or short phrases that indicate what the passage may be addressing. Then I aggregate the codes I have created and scan through them looking for patterns, potential insights, and connections.

Over the years in my reading workshop, I have asked my students to use sticky notes to code texts for two distinct purposes: (1) to indicate sections of a text where they have used a particular reading comprehension strategy so that I can formatively assess how they were implementing the strategies I have taught, and (2) to code texts to highlight particular sections to share or revisit in preparation for literature study discussions.

The ways I have used sticky notes on print-based picture books for documenting reading-comprehension strategies can be done just as easily on digital texts. Using the features built into the digital reading devices, online programs, and mobile apps described below, readers can highlight texts, add written notes, record comments about the reading strategies they are using, make connections to other texts, and keep track of any challenges faced by employing a particular reading strategy. In essence, these digital annotating resources can be used by readers as recording devices for *thinking aloud* about the reading strategies they employ. Teachers can use these written notes and audio recordings to evaluate whether their lessons are having a positive effect on readers' strategy use or whether a particular skill needs to be revisited.

When I have asked my students to code texts in preparation for literature discussions, I have been explicit about the types of codes and comments I've asked them to record. Although I don't tell students exactly what to write down on their notes, I do offer them several categories of possible codes to consider and support for how to code texts while they are reading. In addition, I always provided numerous examples from my own readings or from my former students' readings to help my readers get a sense of what is being required of them. A detailed lesson for supporting students' coding of texts is included later in the chapter.

We have to be explicit and transparent with our students about why we are asking them to code texts, no matter whether they are reading print-based or digital texts. For example, I always explained that reading in preparation for a discussion is different from reading simply for enjoyment. I don't take sticky notes or a highlighter with me to the beach in the summer to mark up my pleasure reading, although I do often make notes in the margin of my books even when I am reading for pleasure. I don't want my readers to be preoccupied with coding when they are simply enjoying a book for themselves. However, preparing for the rigors and expectations associated with literature discussions is different. It's hard to remember everything from a 200-page novel that readers may want to share in their discussion groups. It is because of the requirements associated with these discussions that I require readers to mark up or code texts.

Literature study is a more intensive form of reading than pleasure reading. It requires close attention not only to the story itself but also to the ways in which the author rendered the story, the language used, the writer's craft and style, various literary and narrative elements, themes, and connections to one's life and the world around us. For more ideas on literature discussion groups, I refer you to my previous books on the reading workshop as well as Peterson and Eeds' (1990) classic text, *Grand Conversations*.

In summary, before we teach readers how to use the highlighting and commentary features on digital reading devices we need to be clear about the reasons for doing so in the first place. Most importantly, readers need to understand our expectations for effectively preparing for literature discussion groups. Being well prepared to share one's ideas with other readers forms the impetus for coding and commenting on texts, not simply creating a lesson plan and passing out sticky notes.

Web-Based and Digital Resources for Coding and Commenting on Texts

Here we will focus on the various features found on digital reading devices and computers for highlighting text, generating comments, and sharing comments online with other readers. In addition, I will present a number of apps that can be used for highlighting, writing comments, and sharing these notations on PDFs and other digital files. Some of these apps are available for free online, and others can be purchased through the iTunes or Google Play stores for less than a few dollars. The various apps described here may offer different features for marking up texts—audio-recording notes, capturing digital images and attaching them to a text, and drawing notes in the margins of texts—but all of the devices and apps mentioned have highlighting and commenting capabilities.

Commenting Using Features on a Digital Reading Device

Probably the easiest way to comment on digital texts is by using the built-in features available on various digital reading devices. Kindle Reader, Sony Reader, Nook, Kobo eReader, and iPad all have commenting capabilities. Basically, all of these digital reading devices allow readers to highlight sections of text, look up words in a built-in dictionary, share highlighted sections of texts when connected to the Internet, or review what others have said about particular passages. In addition, most of these digital reading devices—the Kindle Reader for example—allows readers to post highlighted sections of text on their Facebook and Twitter accounts. Digital reading devices that have Wi-Fi compatibility (most include this as a basic feature now) can search the Internet for definitions, author interviews, and other resources to support their readings and interpretations.

In addition to the commenting features of these devices, most of them can aggregate the highlighted sections or comments that a reader has generated into one digital file for reviewing them as a collection. This feature allows readers to review their various highlights and comments, making it easier to see what they have attended to as they were reading. Readers can then decide which, if any, of these highlights or comments they would like to share online. Teachers should refer to the online or built-in manual for how to access these features on selected digital reading devices.

Commenting Using Online and Computer-Based Programs

In addition to the features included on digital reading devices themselves, various online programs and platforms are available for highlighting and commenting on digital texts and sharing these notes with other readers. Most of these programs require readers to create an online account and offer free (lite) versions, with premium versions available that can be purchased or subscribed to for a monthly fee. Most of these programs are used for reading and aggregating online content and allow readers to mark up this digital content with comments and make connections to other online content.

In addition to aggregating online content, Citelighter.com features annotation, citation, and bibliographic capabilities. Citelighter is advertised as a research and writing tool that allows readers to aggregate highlighted and selected content from online sources and attach notes and citation information to these captured files. This program can also connect to Google Docs, allowing readers to import notes directly into a Microsoft Word document.

Citelighter is an excellent tool for reading expository texts online and taking notes for a research project. It allows readers to search the web and aggregate information for a research project or for a piece of argumentative or persuasive writing. The program can create bibliographies in a variety of reference styles. The free version provides a *plug-in*, or extension, to be incorporated into a web browser—Safari, Chrome, Internet Explorer, and Firefox are some examples—for one-button capture of online sources. The Citelighter Pro version has additional features and is available for $10 a month (or $80 a year) at the time of this writing.

I have used another valuable program, Evernote, which is available across computer platforms. It allows for sharing texts, images, and web content via a free, subscription-based online account. Evernote is a business software program that was designed for note taking, highlighting, and sharing presentations. It allows readers to create notes and organize them into a variety of user-generated notebooks that can be archived and shared with other Evernote account holders. It also allows users to sync notebooks and notes across mobile devices and different computers. The basic Evernote program is free to download and use, and a premium version is offered for approximately $50 a year. Evernote also has an associated mobile app for use on smartphones and tablets.

Evernote allows readers to capture screenshots of web pages and online content, add audio recordings to captured files, hyperlink notes to other web addresses and online content, and then aggregate these notes and recordings into specified notebooks. In the classroom, teachers could use this program, and others like it, to create and archive demonstrations of how to use particular online resources as well as provide support for students' research projects and presentations.

These online and computer-based programs help readers navigate the overwhelming amount of information found on the Internet, organize selected content into notebooks, and connect to Google Docs for creating reports and pieces of argument and persuasive writing. Teachers can use these note-taking programs in a variety of ways to support reading and writing workshop activities.

Commenting Using Apps on Mobile Devices

In addition to online, computer, and browser-based programs, there are numerous apps available for mobile devices such as smartphones and tablets that allow readers to highlight, comment on, and aggregate a variety of digital texts, including eBooks, PDFs, images, and web pages. In general, these apps allow readers to import a text, highlight specific sections, type in comment boxes, hand-write notes in the margins, aggregate these highlights and notes, and share them with other readers online.

For the past few years, I have been trying out a variety of note-taking apps and have found GoodReader, Notes Plus, and Notability to be the easiest apps for importing texts (I use mainly PDFs) and adding highlights and comments. Depending on whether you are on an Android, Apple, or other mobile device, these note-taking apps offer similar features and capabilities and are easy to navigate once you spend some time working with them. There are many note-taking apps available online in the iTunes and Google Play stores. Again, I suggest beginning with the basic or free versions of these note-taking apps before investing in the full or premium versions.

GoodReader seems to be the most advanced of the three apps I am describing here. It offers a range of highlighting, annotation, and sharing features. Let me take you through how I have used this app on my tablet (iPad) and offer some ideas for using these apps in the classroom. I have used GoodReader primarily to annotate and comment on PDF files of journal articles. The GoodReader app requires a Wi-Fi or Bluetooth connection for adding content from one's computer onto the tablet or mobile device. After digital texts have been imported into the app, readers can add notes, comments, drawings, audio recordings, and images to the document.

In this app, the main menu is accessible by tapping on the screen of my tablet, and it offers the following capabilities:

- ▸ Highlighted sections of text can be aggregated and shared.
- ▸ Bookmarks can be added to particular pages.
- ▸ Attached annotations or comments can be aggregated and shared.
- ▸ The text of the document can be searched for particular keywords.
- ▸ Arrows, boxes, circles, and markers can be added to call attention to sections of texts or images.
- ▸ Notes and annotations can be compiled into a file that can be uploaded or emailed.

I have used this app to demonstrate to students how I annotate and closely read a particular text, how I mark sections to revisit them, and how I make analytical notes in the margins of these texts. The GoodReader app could easily be used by students to take notes, add comments, and share highlighted sections with other readers in a literature study group or for a research project. The *sync* features in GoodReader allow readers to upload and share notes about a document while reading it at different times and in different places.

Notes Plus and Notability are additional note-taking apps that can be used in a variety of ways to read, highlight, annotate, and share ideas across readers and settings. The Notability and Notes Plus apps allow readers to upload PDFs and other digital content directly from one's Dropbox accounts. This makes importing digital content really easy.

Dropbox is a program and associated app that allows readers to store documents and digital content on a remote server and then access it from a variety of computers and mobile devices. It offers free accounts that provide approximately five gigabytes of space, with more storage space available with a premium subscription. Google Drive and Apple's new Cloud Drive also work in similar fashion.

Penultimate and Skitch are two more of my recommended note-taking and annotation apps. Both of these mobile apps are part of the Evernote suite of apps, and they sync with one's Evernote account for sharing highlights, comments, and screenshots. These apps allow me to import a PDF version of a text, highlight it, add comments, draw arrows on it, circle sections of text, hand-draw notes in the margin, and share these annotations with other readers. These apps require an Evernote account, and they offer basic and premium versions of each app for working with various documents and images.

In addition, many of these note-taking apps allow readers to create audio recordings of a lesson or their own ideas, take pictures of classroom objects and attach them to the digital text, and aggregate and share these annotated files with others. I recommend that you start with the free versions of these apps when available, play around with the various features offered on each app, find one you like, and spend time getting to know its capabilities.

Web-Based and Digital Resources for Discussing Texts

There are basically two kinds of resources for supporting discussion: (1) video-networking programs and apps that allow readers to send text messages, see one another, or simply talk to other readers through an online platform or video feed simultaneously (synchronous discussions) and (2) programs and apps that allow readers to post ideas online and archive them, and allow other readers to respond to them when they have time (asynchronous discussions).

Resources for Synchronous Discussions

Video conferencing software and apps, which were originally designed for business networking purposes, can be used to connect readers in real time with other readers who are connected to the Internet or a Wi-Fi network. The most universally accessible program is Skype, which requires readers to register for a free account and can be used on a variety of computers, smartphones, and tablets. Readers can connect to other readers from around the world and share audio or video feeds to discuss books and ideas. Skype is available as a computer program or as an app for mobile devices. It is free, but has poor quality at times, and readers can experience *drop-offs* at high peak use times.

FaceTime is an Apple app and software program that allows anyone using an Apple iPad, iPhone, or computer to connect free of charge to other Apple users. The video and audio quality of FaceTime is superior to Skype, but it is limited to Apple users. In addition, Google Hangouts, which requires registering for a free Google Plus account, allows readers to connect online to discuss what they have been reading. In addition to talking to one another, these resources also allow participants to bring in video clips, images, and links to websites that everyone could consider together to add to their discussions.

In general, each of these programs or apps requires a digital camera, an Internet connection, and a digital microphone. Also, school firewalls can create barriers for using these video programs in some settings, and working with technology support staff to access these resources may be required. Each of these platforms has its particular features, modes for connecting, and affordances and limitations. Although accessing other readers may have its challenges, the benefits of talking with a variety of other readers from inside and outside one's classroom cannot be overstated.

Resources for Asynchronous Discussions

In previous chapters, I have mentioned web-based resources for searching, reviewing, and recommending books, in particular Goodreads, Amazon, Barnes & Noble, Shelfari, LibraryThing, and others. Some of these sites, in particular Goodreads, also offer platforms for discussing books in chatrooms or online discussion boards. Since I occasionally refer to Goodreads throughout this book, I will share how I have used this resource to set up online discussions with my elementary and college students. Other platforms and websites offer similar capabilities and features, so I will provide a list of some of the ones I have reviewed and found helpful for use in the classroom.

Goodreads requires registering for a free account and an Internet connection. Once registered, readers can archive the books they have read or want to read on digital bookshelves, create wishlists of books to read, read book reviews, connect to other readers, and participate in book discussions by creating their own group or joining a discussion already in progress. I have created discussion groups for my college classes and elementary students. It is very easy to create a group and invite friends to join—simply follow the directions provided on the Goodreads website. Once a group has been created, discussion boards can be set up that focus on particular topics or particular books, and other group members can be invited to add comments or respond to what others have posted.

Other easy-to-use online resources for discussing books are www.pbs.org/parents/education/reading-language/reading-tips/book-clubs-for-kids/ and Al Roker's Book Clubs for Kids at today.com. Each of these sites requires readers to create a free account and register for the book clubs or discussions available. Another online resource that supports readers' sharing of ideas about a particular book or topic is wikispaces.com. This site requires registering for a free account and allows teachers access to a platform for organizing discussions and projects. This resource requires some navigational skill, and I advise watching the online tutorials for learning how to set up one's classroom page. When it is all set up, it is relatively easy to generate a code for students to use to join a group discussion.

One of the challenges associated with asynchronous discussion platforms is ensuring that readers add posts and read what others have added on a regular basis. My review of some of the smaller book club online resources reveals that some book discussions have not been active for quite a while. However, the book discussions on Goodreads are quite active; many readers around the world add ideas in various discussion groups on a regular basis. If you are setting up discussion boards for your classroom, remember that it takes longer to type ideas into a website than it does to sit together and talk. Although these discussion boards may not be the most efficient ways to talk about books, they do provide opportunities to hear from other readers who one might never have the chance to interact with.

Like the concerns I have mentioned in other chapters about responding to one's reading with online and digital tools, I want to be sure that the resources we use to facilitate annotating and discussing books and digital content are efficient and effective compared to the pencil-and-paper tools we have used for many years. If setting up an online discussion board takes too much time away from reading and discussing, it may be best to forego the new technologies in favor of the old ones. New technologies should help teachers and readers do things more efficiently and offer possibilities that analog resources do not. When they don't, their use should be reconsidered.

There are many apps and resources available for highlighting and commenting on digital texts. It is important to learn to navigate the features of the apps and reading devices we use so that the features don't interfere with the processes of reading and thinking. Again here, if using a particular technology gets in the way of reading and discussing, it may be best to go back to using sticky notes. The technology should support the instructional approach or purpose, not the other way around.

Over the years I have used online discussion boards with varying effectiveness in my classrooms. When my elementary students shared their ideas online with their pen pals from Australia, online discussions were all I could provide. My students enjoyed hearing what their friends from other countries thought about the books they were reading. When I have used them as part of my undergraduate and graduate children's literature classes, some students enjoyed discussing the novels they were reading online, and others said they prefer face-to-face interactions. For me, the key has been to offer a variety of options for my students and let them decide the best way to discuss what they are reading, and to see the possibilities and challenges in bringing technology into the reading workshop.

Explicit Lessons for Commenting on and Discussing Digital Texts

The lessons in this chapter focus on resources for annotating texts with highlights and comments that can be revisited and shared in digital environments. In addition, lessons that focus on supporting online discussions and how to participate in an online literature study are included.

Lesson #1 Supporting Readers' Coding of Text

Rationale: Asking readers to add comments and codes to a book, whether print-based or digital, requires teachers to explain the purposes for this practice, and how these codes and comments will be used to enhance discussion.

Objective: Readers will learn how to code or annotate a text to call attention to or comment on particular sections or concepts they want to share in their literature study discussions.

Demonstration: Teachers will share and discuss reasons for coding texts and adding comments, possible categories of the kinds of things to code and annotate, how to aggregate these notes for reviewing them, and how to share them online with other readers.

Resources: Refer to the various digital reading devices, online annotation programs, and mobile apps for note taking discussed in this chapter.

Comments: Figure 6.2 provides a list of possible things readers may code when reading fictional texts.

Lesson #2 Supporting Quality Online Literature Discussions

Rationale: Teachers should not assume that readers know how to talk with other readers about books, whether in face-to-face or online environments. Sharing expectations, offering examples, and demonstrating what is required in a literature discussion are important scaffolds for young readers regardless of where the discussion takes place.

Objective: Readers will discuss various expectations and procedures for ensuring quality literature discussions and create a chart of things that might help and hinder their discussions.

Figure 6.2 Possible Codes for Reading Fictional Texts

- Noticings: Things readers notice as they are reading, including illustrations, language, book design elements, or genre characteristics
- Connections: Things readers connect to themselves from personal experiences or connections to other literary texts
- Interpretations: Potential meanings associated with what the reader notices, including character motives, inferences about themes, mood, symbols, or social issues
- Strategies: Strategies that readers notice they are using to make sense of the text
- Wonderings: Questions readers have
- Confusions: Things that readers find confusing
- Narrative elements: Aspects of the plot, setting, or characters that seem relevant to understanding the story
- Literary devices: Aspects of the writer's style or craft, including figurative language and metaphors

---

Demonstration: By bringing in other teachers to discuss a particular book, or by selecting a group of students who have had previous experiences with literature discussions, the teacher will model what a quality discussion look likes in a face-to-face environment. After creating a list of Helpers and Blockers (see Figure 6.3), students will talk about how these ideas can be used to enhance their online literature discussions.

Resources:
- readinggroupchoices.com—for ideas about conducting online and face-to-face book clubs
- Grand Conversations (Peterson and Eeds 1990)

Comments: There are numerous resources for conducting and supporting literature discussions but very few for facilitating them in online environments. The role of the teacher in these discussions remains one of facilitator, although teachers may end up facilitating the technical aspects of these discussions as much as the literary dimensions.

Setting clear expectations and discussing online etiquette is vital for the success of online discussions. Requiring students to post a certain number of comments each week, responding to other group members a certain number of times, demonstrating what a quality comment or response looks like, and monitoring these discussions are important expectations for online discussions. I have pulled group ideas together by summarizing the online discussion up to a point and posted the summary for readers to consider. In

---

Figure 6.3 Discussion Helpers and Blockers

Helpers do the following:

- Ask other students some questions
- Listen and care about what others think and say
- Make connections to other readers' ideas
- Share resources for digging deeper into a text (i.e., author interviews and websites)
- Give everyone a chance to talk
- Learn to politely disagree
- Refer to the text for possible evidence of interpretations

Blockers do the following:

- Play around in groups and be rude
- Make too many predictions
- Constantly interrupt others
- Allow one person to do all the talking
- Don't come to the group and share ideas
- Say they are done when there may be more to say

---

addition, I read what students have been talking or writing about and set agendas for future discussion based on students' responses and comments up to that point.

Finally, the one experience that has supported online discussions in my classes the most has been my own participation in an online literature discussion group on Goodreads. By actually having to post and respond to readers I have never met, I have experienced the possibilities and challenges of these online resources firsthand. Remember that by participating in online discussions ourselves we can more effectively demonstrate to our students how it all works.

Lesson #3 Virtual Author and Illustrator Visits

Rationale: It can be expensive to have an author or illustrator visit a school or classroom. Instead, by visiting an author or illustrator's website and finding interesting resources about him or her online—through webcasts, podcasts, interviews, book reviews, and biographical posts—teachers can bring authors and illustrators into their classroom virtually via the Internet for little or no money.

Objective: Readers will learn how to research and analyze various online resources pertaining to particular authors and illustrators. The class will gather all potential resources and consider the ways these resources might affect their literature discussions and their interpretations of the books they have been reading.

Demonstration: The teacher will select a favorite author or illustrator and demonstrate how to search online resources for interesting and relevant information about the selected author or illustrator's life, craft, artwork, publications, creative influences, and so forth.

Resources:
- readingrockets.org—has author interviews and videos
- scholastic.com—features hundreds of author videos and interviews
- nbclearn.com—offers videos of children's authors talking to children
- childrensbooks.about.com—features many resources for literacy educators, including author and illustrator interviews and videos

Comments: Making connections among the online resources and the discussions of the books being read in class is key to this lesson. When searching the Internet, teachers will need to decide what is relevant and what is superfluous, and then they can share with students their criteria for selecting what is important. This is a first step in analyzing online information.

CHAPTER SEVEN

Interpreting and Analyzing Digital Texts

The move from a summary of events to a discussion of the meaning or theme of a work of fiction is usually a move from reading to interpretation.

—Robert Scholes, 1985

As theories supporting literacy education have expanded in the past few decades, the text as the primary focus of interpretation and analysis has shifted to include analysis of the reader, the author-illustrator, and the immediate and sociocultural contexts of the reading event. In other words, we cannot simply look at the text *in a vacuum* when trying to understand what it means. We must consider where and when a text was created and why it was distributed. We must consider the conditions under which a text is read or received—for example, the difference between reading a book for a college class and reading it for pleasure. We must consider the author(s) who wrote, illustrated, designed, and published a book. We must take into account the historical, political, and sociocultural influences that affected its production. We must consider who is reading the book, under what conditions, and for what purposes. And, of course, we must consider the textual, visual, and design elements of the text itself. As we move from simply *reading words* to *interpretation and analysis*—as alluded to in the opening epigraph—we must focus on understanding how readers generate meaning from both a physical text and a larger cultural text (Scholes 1985).

In the three previous chapters, I began by distinguishing between the processes included in the title of each chapter, noting, for example, the differences between accessing and navigating (Chapter 4), archiving and sharing (Chapter 5), and commenting and discussing (Chapter 6). In this chapter, the focus is on the connections between the processes of interpreting and analyzing, not the differences. These two processes differ simply by a matter of degree: Interpreting and analyzing are both aspects of a single process—thinking critically about texts. The process of *interpreting and analyzing* has always sounded as though it is a deeper, more reflective process than simply reading. We must explore the implications for this type of deeper reading.

Many of the strategies I have shared previously with students during my reading workshops, those that support their responses to and analyses of texts, can be easily transferred to digital or online platforms. By shifting various analytical approaches and discussion strategies into the digital age, we make them available to a wider audience and allow for collaboration among students in new and exciting ways. Charts that used to hang on my classroom walls can now be posted online for other teachers and students to review and consider. Breaking down classroom walls in this way is the most exciting aspect of moving to the reading workshop 2.0 environment.

Close Reading or Analytical Reading?

In the past few years, reading teachers have been asked to help students read texts *more closely*. Commonly referred to as *close reading*, this way of reading has been rejuvenated by the emergence of the Common Core State Standards. To address these new standards, readers are asked to read closely to (1) determine what the text says explicitly, (2) make logical inferences from their interactions with a text, and (3) cite specific textual evidence when writing or speaking to support their conclusions drawn from the text. This focus on what is directly stated in the text requires readers to read closely, paying special attention to the language and structure of texts; to various elements of literature, such as plot, character, and setting; to figures of speech such as metaphors and symbols; and to the use of symbols, motifs, and literary archetypes. A cursory review of the Common Core State Standards (corestandards.org) reveals an emphasis on the text itself, moving away from the influences of the reader, the author, the illustrator, and the sociocultural context.

In addition to supporting the strategies involved in close reading, the web-based and digital resources included in this chapter can be used to help readers interpret and analyze all four dimensions of the act of reading: author-illustrator, text, reader, and context. For purposes of this chapter, the strategy labeled *close reading* will be considered only one strategy for interpreting and analyzing texts. In contrast to close reading, I prefer the term *analytical reading*, which includes close reading of the text itself and strategies that consider the text as only one source of information to be analyzed along with the author, illustrator and designer, publisher, sociocultural factors, and the actual reader involved in the act of reading.

In the process of interpreting and analyzing a text, both *textual* (written language, visual images, and design) factors that are in the text itself and *contextual* (author, publisher, reader, cultural, and societal) factors that are outside the actual text need to be considered. The web-based and digital resources presented in this chapter will focus on both textual and contextual factors that readers should consider when interpreting and analyzing texts in the reading workshop 2.0.

Resources for Considering Textual Factors

Many print-based, digital, and web-based resources may be useful for supporting readers' interpretations and analysis of texts. Drawing on Web 2.0 technologies, the resources in this section are used to call close attention to the various elements of multimodal texts—namely written language, visual images, and graphic designs—and the connections among these elements. I will begin with resources that take a broad overview for analyzing multimodal texts, meaning that they consider all elements of the text, before sharing resources that can be used to focus on particular elements in relative isolation.

Charts and Visual Representations

I have been using the chart presented in Figure 7.1 to call readers' attention to the three essential elements of print-based or digital multimodal texts. This chart is designed primarily to get readers to consider visual images and design elements in addition to the written text. Readers are to consider the three elements of a multimodal text, listed across the top of the chart, by asking themselves the three questions listed down the left-hand side. We want readers to notice and analyze all aspects of digital and web-based multimodal texts, not just the written words.

This chart can be created on a sheet of chart paper or by using one of the following digital resources for visual representation, or *mind-mapping*. The web-based and digital programs and apps presented in this section allow paper charts to leave the walls of the classroom and be created and posted online so that ideas can be reviewed and revised by a number of students, at different times and from different devices.

Figure 7.1 Text, Image, and Design Analysis Chart

	Written Text	**Visual Images**	**Design Elements**
What do I notice?			
What might it mean?			
What am I wondering?			

The program Cacoo.com allows teachers to create graphs and diagrams that can be added to by other users. In addition to the text, image, and design analysis chart shown in Figure 7.1, I have used Cacoo to create double-entry journals and other visual representations to support my students' analysis and discussions of a text. These digitally rendered charts allow readers to *drag and drop* direct quotes or visual images from a book on one side of the chart and then react to what they posted on the other side. Cacoo allows user-created visual representations to be posted online so students can add entries to their charts over time. By making the text-image-design chart, double-entry journal, or other visual representation available online, students are able to review and collaborate from wherever they have access to the Internet, not just during class time.

Another web-based program that allows teachers and students to collaborate on a visual representation, or *mind-map*, is called Popplet.com. This online website allows teachers and students to collaboratively create graph "bubbles" that connect to one another and to central ideas. This visual representation allows readers to add their interpretations to a collaborative mind-map. Readers can review what their classmates have added to the visual display and then add their own thoughts. This online resource also has an app version for use on a mobile device. Other online resources that offer similar visual representation or mind-mapping capabilities are bubbl.us, mindmeister.com, and drichard.org/mindmaps.

I have used these digital resources to support several reading and discussion strategies that I have advocated for in my print-based reading workshops. For example, *word storms* are a discussion and analysis strategy that asks readers to write down ten words that come to mind as I read a book aloud. Each reader chooses three words from their word storm list that come directly from the book or from their thoughts and then writes a brief reflection of his or her reasons for choosing those three words. The class discusses their choices and reasoning in small groups or as a whole class. The digital resources just described could easily support this discussion strategy. Classes could use any of the visual representation platforms to collaboratively create a word storm that features words from the entire group.

Another web-based resource that can be used to visually represent the frequency of particular words in a text is called Wordle. This is an online resource that allows you to cut and paste any digital text into its website, and then it calculates the frequency of the words in the text. Figure 7.2 is an example of a Wordle I created from the complete text of my first book from Heinemann, *The Reading Workshop: Creating Space for Readers*. This visual representation shows the words that occur the most frequently as the largest. It is interesting to discover which words were used the most, and the least, throughout my book.

This resource could also be used to get a sense of what was talked about the most in a literature study group discussion. For example, if we transcribed a group discussion and submitted it to Wordle, we might end up with a visual

Figure 7.2 Wordle of *The Reading Workshop* Book

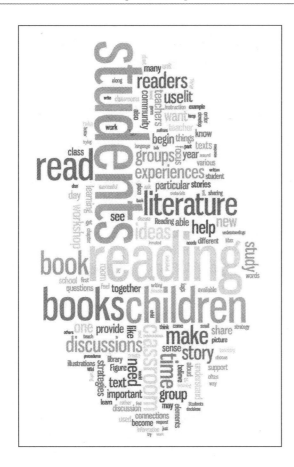

Figure 7.3 Wordle of *The Hunger Games* Discussion

representation like the one in Figure 7.3. This Wordle comes from a discussion of Suzanne Collins' book, *The Hunger Games*, by a group of fifth graders.

By looking at this visual representation, it is very easy to see what words were used the most when students discussed *The Hunger Games* and what topics might be important to return to for further consideration. Wordle is a quick and easy resource for finding the frequency of words in any digital text.

One additional analytical tool I have used for discussing how a character changes over time in a novel or picture book is a *character timeline*. It is more important to discuss and analyze how a character changes across a narrative than to be able to describe particular aspects of the character, like we used to do by drawing character webs. There are many online resources for creating a timeline. Some free and relatively simple ones to explore are dipity.com, time-glider.com, ourstory.com, and timetoast.com. Each of these has a free version and premium options that provide more resources and capabilities.

Digital Storyboards

Another app or online resource that I have used to help readers look at the design of picture books during their analysis are storyboards. I have displayed the print-based pages of various picture books, for example, *Where the Wild Things Are* (Sendak 1963), *Voices in the Park* (Browne 2001), and *Black and White* (Macauley 1990) across the walls of my classroom. After displaying the pages from a picture book across the classroom wall on butcher paper, we wrote down ideas and drew arrows and symbols on the paper as we discussed and analyzed the story and images. This display became a visual representation that was created collaboratively during our analysis of these picture books.

It would be very easy to use one of the storyboard apps or online platforms to simulate the same display in digital form, allowing readers to add comments and visual images to the storyboard from their computers or mobile devices. A quick search online reveals that there are numerous templates available for creating storyboards. Many of these programs and apps allow readers to drag and drop images directly into the storyboard boxes. An excellent online resource for creating digital storyboards is *storyboardthat.com*. StoryboardThat offers a free version of the program as well as premium versions for a monthly fee. A good resource for suggestions and ideas about how to create digital storyboards is digitalstorytelling.coe.uh.edu. Digital storyboarding can be used in the writing workshop as a way to plan narrative stories as well.

There are other resources that provide support for creating digital stories that allow users to add visual images, video recordings, background music, and sound effects to a storyboard and then produce a digital story in various formats. Most of them are simple to use and include tutorials on their websites. Students' drawings, written texts, and images from picture books can be easily uploaded and added to their stories. Other easy-to-use and inexpensive resources are storify.com, littlebirdtales.com, zooburst.com, storybird.com, and fuzzwich.com.

Digital Bulletin Boards

Another type of web-based resource allows users to *clip and post* web pages, images, text, and other digital sources and arrange them in visual displays that can be shared with other users. Two of the most popular digital bulletin board websites are Instagram and Pinterest. These two programs allow users to create accounts, clip and pin images from websites and other sources, and give other users the opportunity to follow their postings. They may contain content that is not suitable for some students, though, because they are open to adults.

Other digital bulletin board programs and apps allow users to limit who can post and see individual bulletin boards, and these resources may be more appropriate for classroom use. A few of the more popular ones are Padlet, Flipgrid, Lino, and eduClipper. Flipgrid and Lino also provide an app version for clipping and posting from mobile devices. These programs and apps provide a digital canvas for users to post web pages, written notes, images, and other digital documents, and then arrange them into categories for sharing online. In addition, Padlet provides an extension for installing a button in your web browser that makes it even easier to clip web pages, text boxes, and images into your online canvas.

These resources could be used to create digital bulletin boards, allowing students to post items of interest. Or, they could be used to focus attention on a particular topic or book, and students can post clippings that pertain to the topic. For example, I used these digital bulletin board programs and apps for students to visualize ideas after reading a poem. I posted the poem on the canvas platform and let students post or draw images that reflected what was in their mind as they read the poem. These displays were then used as a foundation for further discussion and analysis of the poem. I have also used a digital bulletin board app to collect research on a particular topic. Students clip images and other web content to a collective bulletin board and use this display as an organizing tool for writing research papers.

Another interesting resource that can be used for collaborative thinking and visual representation are *digital whiteboards*. These web-based programs and apps for mobile devices provide a blank whiteboard and digital markers for users to draw freehand anything they want. Students could use these whiteboards to respond to their readings by picturing the setting from a poem or story and then drawing it. They could use them as *digital graffiti boards*, with symbols and sketches that represent their understandings of a story or expository text. Other educators have referred to this strategy as a *sketch-to-stretch* activity. Three of the online programs I have used are educreations.com (which also provides an app version for mobile devices), cosketch.com, and draw.to. All of these resources allow multiple users to collaboratively add to a blank whiteboard and display and share their work with other students.

Graphica Software

There are some great resources, both online programs and app versions, that allow users to create texts that simulate cartoons, comics, and graphic novels, what Thompson (2008) calls *graphica*. Aside from their obvious use in supporting students in the writing workshop, I have used these as analysis tools in both print-based and digital formats. In my print-based reading workshop, I asked readers to place thought-shaped or speech-bubble sticky notes on images in picture books and then write what they believe the character might be thinking or saying. What students wrote on the sticky notes were examples of the inferences they drew from reading the text. It was a great way to demonstrate inferential thinking.

Doing this with any graphica software available today is so much easier and, of course, allows us to display responses online and share them across groups of students. I have used three online resources to create comics and graphic novel displays: toondoo.com, bitstrips.com, and comiclife.com. Toon-Doo is an online platform that allows users to select from available characters and backgrounds to create their own cartoons or comic strips. Bitstrips and Comic Life are both available as online platforms and as apps for mobile devices. I have also used these graphica resources for rearranging story events in different sequences to develop strategies for understanding narrative structures.

I have found that my students really enjoy using these graphica programs and resources, and they have discovered many ways to apply them to their reading and writing experiences.

Digital Reader Response Notebooks

In my print-based reading workshop, I used to provide a notebook for students to respond to our daily read-alouds. This *walking journal* was shared among the readers in my class. It provided a space for individual students to write their ideas and reactions about a book and then read other students' comments and reactions. This would have been so much easier if the digital resources I am sharing here were available back then.

Using shared writing resources like Wikispaces or Google Docs, or any number of blogging websites such as Blogger, WordPress, or Tumblr, I could easily provide a platform for readers to collaboratively share their written responses to their independent readings and our whole-class read-alouds. In Chapter 5 I mentioned various ways the Goodreads platform might be used to share book reviews, commentaries, and recommendations. Readers could certainly use Goodreads, Shelfari, and LibraryThing to collaboratively respond to what they have read and share their ideas online. One advantage of doing the walking journal in digital format is that I could review and assess my students' ideas from home without hauling around a box of notebooks.

Lots of support is required when we introduce response notebooks to our students. We need to model for students not only what types of content to include in their responses but also how to post them online, find other students' responses, and add to their friends' commentaries. Over the years there was one thing I could count on: Every student's book reviews and response notebook entries improved as we worked with this writing genre throughout the year.

Screencasts

Screencasts are programs and apps that can capture what is on a computer screen as an individual image or as a video recording. Screencasts can be very helpful when showing someone how to do something online or showing someone else what we are looking at on our computer. There are many tutorials found online that demonstrate how to register for a website or how to work with a particular online resource, all of which are created using different screencast programs or apps.

Most screencasting programs are available as both apps and as downloadable programs. Some of the easier-to-use programs that offer free versions, in addition to premium versions, are screencast-o-matic.com, movavi.com, and screenrecord.com. Adobe (the software company that makes Adobe Reader) offers the Captivate program, which works with the Adobe suite of software tools.

Captivate is a much more extensive program than most teachers would need to make simple screencast images or short video clips, but it also offers annotating and other options and support.

TechSmith (techsmith.com) offers a variety of video and screen-capture software programs and apps. The most sophisticated (and the most expensive at ninety-nine dollars) is Camtasia. This program supports professional-level video capture and editing capabilities and is probably more advanced than most teachers will need. However, TechSmith also offers a suite of individual software tools called Snagit, Screencast, and Jing. I have been using the free program Jing for several years to capture images and create videos from my computer screen. It allows me to create images of my computer screen and add arrows, text boxes, and other annotations to call students' attention to various elements on my screen.

Using Screencast, another program from TechSmith, I can upload the videos and images I capture to my social media accounts, like Facebook, Twitter, and Blogger. For most classroom uses, Jing offers plenty of capabilities and annotating options.

I have used screencasting programs and apps in several ways in my reading workshop. First, I have used the video-capture capabilities to show students how to register for a Goodreads account and to demonstrate how to use other online resources. It is much easier to click a button, video-record yourself talking as you work through registering procedures online, and post these videos so students can watch what you did rather than trying to type out the directions. Second, I have used screencasting programs to demonstrate how to write a book review or reading response journal entry. I simply start the video-capture program and start talking aloud as I write and revise my reviews. My students can then revisit these demonstration lessons later. The Jing program is great for capturing your think-alouds on video so students can revisit any lessons you taught.

Finally, I have used screencasts to capture my thought processes as I analyze a particular text or image. Jing allows me to open up a scanned image from a picture book on my computer and share my analytical processes with students. I can use the annotation and recording options to show students how I approach an image and share the thoughts going through my head as I look at it. I can record my initial noticings and work through the process of interpreting an image, adding arrows and highlights to the image or text and placing written notes on the image. Then I can share my ideas with my students face to face or post them online for further review. Figure 7.4 shows an example of what an annotated image from *Voices in the Park* might look like.

Additional Audiovisual Resources

There are many additional resources for adding music and sound effects to images and texts, creating multimodal presentations, capturing video and audio

Figure 7.4 Jing Image Analysis Example

TechSmith product screenshot reprinted with permission from TechSmith Corporation.

recordings, digital storytelling, taking surveys and polls, and producing podcasts. Some of these resources may be familiar to most teachers—PowerPoint, VoiceThread, and Edmodo—and others they may not have heard of. To make teachers aware of the wide variety of programs and apps available, I have included resources for creating visual presentations and audiovisual displays, and for conducting polls and surveys for teachers to explore. For each type of resource, I have included a brief description of their capabilities and suggestions on how these programs and apps might be used in the reading workshop 2.0.

1. Multimodal presentation resources. These resources are designed to support students when creating visual and multimodal presentations. They can be used to present research projects, display the contents of group discussions, and provide support for public speaking. They are PowerPoint (Microsoft), Keynote (Apple), Prezi.com, Glogster.com, Slideshare.com, Photosnack.com, and Knovio.com.

2. Audiovisual recording resources. These resources can be used to create podcasts, create audio or video recordings of students' work and projects, record group literature discussions, record role-playing scenarios such as interviewing a fictional character from a book, and link music to the content and themes of various texts. These

are animoto.com, aurasma.com, ticklypictures.com, audioboo.fm, audiopal.com, vine.co, vinjavideo.com, jamstudio.com, and audacity .sourceforge.net.

3. Surveys and polls. These resources can be used to take polls and create surveys to get a general sense of students' reactions and responses to stories and informational texts. They are pollsevery-where.com, surveymonkey.com, polldaddy.com, and insightify.com.

All of the resources listed so far have focused on the written text, visual images, and design elements of print-based and digital multimodal texts. They can be used to annotate texts and demonstrate close reading techniques for students. Students do not need a lot of time before they feel comfortable using most of these resources, and many may have used some of these resources already. Using our imaginations, these resources can be used in many other ways to support the analysis of texts in the reading workshop. I have also included an extensive list of additional websites and online resources for supporting technology and literacy education in the Appendix.

Resources for Considering Contextual Factors

There are things outside the text itself that must be considered when interpreting a text: the person who is reading, the context in which the reading is taking place, the creator of the text, how the text was distributed, and the social and cultural contexts surrounding the production and reception of these texts.

Consider the Perspectives of Authors and Illustrators

By reading author and illustrator interviews, exploring websites dedicated to the work of a particular author or illustrator, considering biographical information about the people who create the texts we encounter, and studying reviews and critical essays written by children's literature experts, we can expand our perspectives for interpreting and analyzing texts. It's not about the author or the illustrator retaining control over what a text or illustration means; rather, readers should consider the author and illustrators' intentions and the contexts of producing the texts and images.

Now most author-illustrators have a personal website or one created for them by their publishers. Simply searching for an author or illustrator's name in any web browser reveals thousands of these sites that have lists of books they have published, interviews they have given, notes about their creative processes, and reviews of their work. Many of the sites also contain video clips of the author or illustrator talking about their writing craft or illustration style. You might even find a video that takes readers on a tour of where well-known authors and illustrators write and create their artworks. Although there are too many to list here, and it's very easy to search for authors and illustrators on the Internet, I've listed a few of my favorite websites for finding author-illustrator information in Figure 7.5.

Other Contexts to Consider

Along with information about the author and illustrator, it is important to consider the role of the designer and publisher when analyzing a text. Like it or not, publishing houses determine what we get to read. Children's book publishers and book retailers play a big role in determining what gets published and distributed, what gets put on the shelves of bookstores and classrooms, and what types of books are made available in online bookstores. Ideological factors play a part in determining what gets published. Book publishers and retailers—for example, companies that support environmental and political causes—play a role in determining elementary reading curricula and create materials for teachers to use in the classroom. These are not innocent, objective decisions. We need to be vigilant as we consider what we ask students to read and must provide them with opportunities to consider the ramifications of these decisions on their reading lives.

Figure 7.5 Favorite Author-Illustrator Websites

Collections of Authors and Illustrators

- Harper Collins author-illustrators: harpercollinschildrens.com
- Children's authors and illustrators: ucalgary.ca/~dkbrown/authors.html
- Websites for kids: gws.ala.org/category/literature-amp-languages/authors-illustrators
- Scholastic authors: scholastic.com/teacher/ab/biolist.htm
- Random House: randomhousekids.com

Individual Author and Illustrator Websites

- Chris Van Allsburg: chrisvanallsburg.com
- Jan Brett: janbrett.com
- Brian Selznick: theinventionofhugocabret.com/index.htm
- Graeme Base: graemebase.com
- David Wiesner: davidwiesner.com
- Kevin Henkes: kevinhenkes.com
- Tom Lichtenheld: tomlichtenheld.com
- Jon Scieszka: guysread.com
- James Patterson: readkiddoread.com
- Neil Gaiman: mousecircus.com

In addition to the information provided about authors and illustrators, publishers create advertisements, often in the form of book trailers, in an effort to activate readers' background knowledge and help them anticipate what might happen in a story. Analyzing the advertisements, interviews, press releases, book reviews, and essays that accompany the publication of a book can expand our awareness of the potential meanings associated with a fictional story or expository text.

Finally, a growing genre has become available online for fans of particular books, movies, television shows, and other pop cultural artifacts. Generically referred to as *fanfiction*, it covers a whole range of pop culture texts. Fanfiction stories build upon aspects of the original stories, expanding and adapting various characters, settings, and plots into new stories. On the website fanfiction.net, for example, there are over a half million adaptations of Harry Potter stories. Unlike stories controlled by traditional publishers, an online community of fans regulates fanfiction. Reading these adaptations helps expand students' interpretations and understandings of the original stories.

Understanding the historical context surrounding a book's creation and taking into account the context under which it is read can support readers' further analyses of the text itself. For example, understanding the social context of the United States in 1963 when *Where the Wild Things Are* (Sendak) was published can help readers understand the meanings and challenges associated with this story during that time. Adults were being advised in articles in several parenting magazines not to read this book to children before bedtime for fear of scaring them before going to sleep. The Internet is an excellent place to find this type of historical information about books, eras, and events, which readers to use to expand their interpretations and analyses of the books they are reading.

Understanding the political and historical contexts of producing picture books and novels for children plays an important role in understanding the texts we read in digital and analog environments. The digital age has made it easier to find lots of information associated with the production of the texts we read. Taken as a whole, the resources provided here that focus on the contexts of production and reception of texts, in addition to the resources provided earlier that focus on the text itself, expand our students' interpretive repertoires and the perspectives they are able to bring to the texts they encounter in the reading workshop 2.0.

Explicit Lessons for Interpreting and Analyzing Digital Texts

The final set of lessons provided in this book focus on strategies for analyzing news reports across various sources of information, ways to further engage with fictional characters through social media, and ways to respond to what students read.

Lesson #1 Analyzing News Reports Across Internet Sources

Rationale: An important skill to have in the digital age is the ability to analyze and evaluate the perspective and quality of a news report, along with being able to understand the possible subjectivities, biases, and stereotypes presented. Questioning the authority of informational sources, established organizations, and commercial publishers is vital for evaluating the multiple voices involved in any particular issue. Only through the consideration of a variety of sources can readers begin to analyze the information provided through any single resource.

Objective: Readers will learn how to use different search engines to locate information on a particular topic presented across a variety of web-based resources and how to develop criteria to evaluate that information.

Demonstration: Teachers will use the Save the Pacific Tree Octopus website (http://zapatopi.net/treeoctopus/) to show readers how inaccurate information is often available online. This farcical website has been around since 1998 and is one of the best-known Internet hoaxes. Evaluating the information provided on this site requires searching through other sites because the Tree Octopus is presented as a real endangered animal and no clues to the farce are offered on the site itself. Once this fake resource has been explored, students will take a real news event and look at how it is reported across newspapers and other sources from different countries and across the United States. Blending conservative and progressive news sources from different countries provides a variety of perspectives on any news event.

Resources: There are many news aggregators that can be helpful places to start searching for information, including Fark, Pulse, Feedly, News 360, Google News, Yahoo News, NewsBlur, and all major newspapers (*The New York Times, San Francisco Chronicle, Le Monde, The Guardian, The Moscow Times*, etc.).

Comments: In addition to the different perspectives provided by different news sources, various search engines—duckduckgo.com, blekko.com, bing.com, ziipa.com, and topsy.com—aggregate Internet resources using different algorithms and deliver different results for the same keyword search than Google. Further resources for evaluating media sources are available in *Media Literacy in the K–12 Classroom* (Baker 2012) and *Digital and Media Literacy: Connecting Culture and Classroom* (Hobbs 2011). With the proliferation of information and news sources on the Internet, evaluating the quality of news reports that our students read is important to maintaining democratic principles and preventing our students from falling prey to the perspectives and agendas from any single source of information. The credibility of any source of information on the Internet should not be based on how "official" a website looks or which authors are listed as "experts."

Rather, the credibility of Internet sources must be based on a commitment by readers to analyzing the reliability of the information by considering the perspectives and biases of the publishers of that information.

Lesson #2 Exploring Characters Through Social Media

Rationale: Understanding the role of character and how characters' motives play a part in young readers' narrative fiction increases in importance as these characters become more complex and their motives more ambiguous.

Objective: Readers will create a social media profile for a selected fictional character and respond to other students' comments and posts in the role of their selected character. This activity would work best as an online experience but could also be managed in a print-based environment.

Demonstration: Teachers first create a template for students to fill in and subsequently provide access for other students to respond to the profile. I have begun this activity by asking students about the different types of information they have posted on their own social media platforms (when available). We then created a list of items to be included on the template for our fictional character, and I created a print-based or web-based resource for students to use to create the profile of their selected characters. I started this activity by having students conduct research into a particular character and decide how this character would act and speak. I then invited my students to an informal lunch in our room, during which they each acted like the character they selected, mingling and conversing throughout the lunch period. Of course, because access to social media can be difficult in some settings and student privacy issues must always be taken into consideration, this activity can be conducted online or face-to-face.

Resources: MySpace.com, Facebook.com, Goodreads.com, and other social media sites.

Comments: The biggest challenges with this project are issues of privacy and student anonymity when real social media sites are used. If possible, have the technology staff at your school create a way to post these character profiles on classroom websites or the school's private server to keep students' profiles and postings private. (Many schools have built-in firewalls that don't allow access to MySpace and Facebook or other social media.) The primary focus of this activity should remain on creating the profile of the fictional character and responding to other students as characters. This can be done through paper-and-pencil posters and role-playing exercises as well as through online and school-based social media.

Lesson #3 Multimodal Responses to Children's and Young Adult Literature

Rationale: Having readers respond to their readings through a variety of multimodal and multimedia resources can extend their understandings of a fictional book or informational text by requiring them to transmediate their ideas across modalities. In other words, having readers create a visual representation of a written poem requires them to reconsider the meanings of the poem before representing their interpretations through sketches, paintings, or ink drawings. It is the act of rethinking the meaning potential of a text that is important, not the use of various features of presentation software or programs.

Objective: Readers will respond to a whole-class read-aloud or book from their independent reading using various web-based resources to represent their understandings.

Demonstration: Using an online resource, such as Glogster.com, Prezi.com, or Educreations.com, the teacher will demonstrate how readers have responded to a text and represent their understandings through the programs selected.

Resources: PowerPoint (Microsoft), Keynote (Apple), Prezi.com, Glogster.com, Slideshare.com, Photosnack.com, and Knovio.com. In addition, information on blogging and creating podcasts in response to what students read is available on *Blogs, Wikis, Podcasts, and Other Powerful Web Tools for Classrooms* (Richardson 2009).

Comments: A little of this type of response activity goes a long way. We don't want students to be required to create a presentation every time they finish a book. Sometimes these activities begin to resemble traditional book reports, except they are done online rather than on a sheet of paper. The power of responding across modes is to stretch students' thinking, not to simply prove they read a book.

EPILOGUE: POWERING DOWN!

You can't teach what you don't know, so anyone who doesn't know how to enjoy reading literature, thinking about it, and entering into dialogues about it shouldn't try to teach those pleasures to others.

—Perry Nodelman, 1996

As I sit at my desk contemplating the fact that I have finished my ninth book for literacy educators, the feeling is not quite as satisfying as it has been in the past. Don't get me wrong, it's always fulfilling to finish any writing project. But this one feels different for some reason. I think it's because there are so many other resources I wanted to share and talk about and explore myself that I just didn't have time or space to cover. This book seems more open-ended than my other ones because the digital world and Web 2.0 resources are expanding so fast it's hard to know what will stay and what will disappear. I feel like I was just beginning to explore all the wonderful resources that are now available for educators to draw upon—and now I'm obligated to send in this manuscript for publication.

We come to know those things we enjoy and spend time doing with greater efficiency and speed than those things we despise and pay little attention to. It's just that simple sometimes. If we are afraid to engage with or consider the potential impact that web-based and digital resources could have on our teaching, we won't be successful in the digital age. People may still call for a *back to basics* focus for our curriculum, but we must realize that in the digital age "the basics" have changed dramatically.

As Kylene Beers stated in her foreword to Kist's (2010) *The Socially Networked Classroom*, the wall is still many teachers' primary instructional tool. Although chalkboards and mimeograph machines have given way to smartboards, scanners, and LCD projectors, the basic philosophy remains the same—students are required to fill in the blanks. Just because the fill-in-the-blank worksheet is on a screen instead of a sheet of paper doesn't make it better. To support our students' experiences with web-based and digital resources, we must interact with these resources and texts ourselves.

Teachers can't just read about web-based and digital resources; they have to begin exploring these resources for themselves. Teachers also need to begin thinking about how these resources might be used in their reading workshops.

To help teachers move forward into the digital age, they need to be given time to explore a wide range of digital resources, time to talk with other teachers about how they have been using these resources in their classrooms, and time to play around with them. And they need be able to provide time for their students to play around with them and visualize new ways to use these resources in the reading workshop.

I will be the first to admit that there are challenges to making use of new technologies in the classroom. Teachers' limited experience and familiarity with new technologies as well as limited resources are the first two challenges that come to mind. The lack of resources in some low socioeconomic schools and classrooms, often referred to as the *digital divide*, is a real challenge that needs to be overcome. Maintaining safe environments for our students through the use of firewalls is vital as we expose our students to the Internet. But these challenges must be met head on if we expect to take advantage of the web-based and digital resources available and help our students be successful in the digital age.

For a month last year I kept track of the different types of reading I did every day. My self-study revealed that I read and write extensively in both print-based and digital environments. From daily email and text messages to greeting cards, I consistently used both paper and pencil and digital technologies to support my reading life. I have had no problem giving up some long-held print-based literacy practices in favor of digital technologies when they have proven to be more efficient and effective.

I am the one who decided when my print-based calendar needed to move into the digital age. I am now able to sync my new calendar program with other family members so we can see what everyone has on their schedule. Making the shift from a typewriter to my computer and writing letters as email were easy changes. The advantages of these new technologies were obvious, and the shift was as much a social phenomenon as a personal insight. Yet other new technologies have been more difficult to accept. For example, I still write notes in my paper notebook. The origins of most of this book began in my notebook and on legal pads before being transferred into a digital document. My daily "to-do" list is still on a sheet of paper so I can keep it in my pocket. There are hundreds of digital to-do lists available, but for me the sheet of paper in my pocket is still the most effective and efficient technology.

As a college professor and former elementary teacher, I feel the same way about new technologies in the reading workshop. If the new technologies help me to do something more effectively and efficiently, if the new technology allows my students to work more collaboratively, if it improves my students' reading abilities, well, I am on board. But I am not afraid to say when any of the new technologies are more cumbersome and less efficient. As we move into the digital age, we have to let go of some outdated practices and embrace the new technologies that support our teaching and our students' learning in more effective and efficient ways.

It is my hope that you find the resources in this book helpful as you plan your school year and organize your reading workshop. I also hope you will continue to revisit the resources I have provided on my website, at www.frankserafini.com/rw20.html.

I promise to continually update my website to share with literacy educators the exciting new resources that are made available in the near future. It is now time for you to explore these resources and decide which ones might help you and your students lead literate lives and continue to grow as lifelong readers.

APPENDIX: ADDITIONAL ONLINE EDUCATIONAL RESOURCES

- ▸▸ tech2learn.wikispaces.com
- ▸▸ web20-21stcentury-tools.wikispaces.com
- ▸▸ classroom20.com
- ▸▸ freetech4teachers.com
- ▸▸ educationdive.com
- ▸▸ snacktools.com
- ▸▸ Dr. Richard Beach's website: www.tc.umn.edu/~rbeach/link steachingmedia/index.htm
- ▸▸ Dr. Troy Hicks' website: digitalwritingworkshop.wikispaces.com
- ▸▸ literacy.alltop.com
- ▸▸ educationnews.org
- ▸▸ educreations.com
- ▸▸ readwritethink.org
- ▸▸ edutopia.com
- ▸▸ opened.io
- ▸▸ teachertools.org
- ▸▸ edmodo.com
- ▸▸ moodle.org
- ▸▸ schooltown.net
- ▸▸ voicethread.com

PROFESSIONAL REFERENCES

Asselin, Marlene, and Maryam Moayeri. 2011. "The Participatory Classroom: Web 2.0 in the Classroom." *Australian Journal of Language and Literacy* 19 (2): i–vii.

Baker, Frank W. 2012. *Media Literacy in the K–12 Classroom*. Eugene, OR: International Society for Technology in Education.

Boyd, Danah. 2014. *It's Complicated: The Social Lives of Networked Teens*. New Haven, CT: Yale University Press.

Campbell, Robin. 2001. *Read-Alouds With Young Children*. Newark, DE: International Reading Association.

Castells, Manuel. 2002. *The Internet Galaxy: Reflections on the Internet, Business and Society*. Oxford: Oxford University Press.

Chambers, Aidan. 1996. *Tell Me: Children, Reading, and Talk*. York, ME: Stenhouse.

Dalton, Bridget, and C. Patrick Proctor. 2008. "The Changing Landscape of Text and Comprehension in the Age of New Literacies." In *Handbook of Research on New Literacies*, edited by J. Coiro, M. Knobel, Colin Lankshear, and Donald J. Leu, 297–324. New York: Lawrence Erlbaum Associates.

Davies, Julia, and Guy Merchant. 2009. *Web 2.0 for Schools: Learning and Social Participation*. New York: Peter Lang.

Dresang, Eliza T. 1999. *Radical Change: Books for Youth in a Digital Age*. New York: H. W. Wilson.

Fox, Mem. 2001. *Reading Magic: Why Reading Aloud to Our Children Will Change Their Lives Forever*. San Diego: Harcourt Brace.

Freebody, Peter, and Allan Luke. 1990. "Literacies Programs: Debates and Demands in Cultural Context." *Prospect: Australian Journal of TESOL* 5 (7): 7–16.

Gee, James Paul, and Elisabeth R. Hayes. 2011. *Language and Learning in the Digital Age*. London: Routledge.

Hicks, Troy. 2009. *The Digital Writing Workshop*. Portsmouth, NH: Heinemann.

Hobbs, Renee. 2011. *Digital and Media Literacy: Connecting Culture and Classroom*. Thousand Oaks, CA: Corwin Press.

Javorsky, Kristin, and Guy Trainin. 2014. "Teaching Young Readers to Navigate a Digital Story When Rules Keep Changing." *The Reading Teacher* 67 (8): 606–618.

Jenkins, Henry, Sam Ford, and Joshua Green. 2013. *Spreadable Media: Creating Value and Meaning in a Networked Culture*. New York: New York University Press.

Johnson, Denise. 2014. *Reading, Writing, and Literacy 2.0: Teaching with Online Texts, Tools, and Resources, K–8*. New York: Teachers College Press.

Joosten, Tanya. 2012. *Social Media for Educators: Strategies and Best Practices*. San Francisco: Jossey-Bass.

Kist, William. 2010. *The Socially Networked Classroom: Teaching in the New Media Age*. Thousand Oaks, CA: Corwin Press.

Kress, Gunther. 2010. *Multimodality: A Social Semiotic Approach to Contemporary Communication*. London: Routledge.

Lankshear, Colin, and Michele Knobel. 2006. *New Literacies: Everyday Practices and Classroom Learning*. Berkshire, UK: Open University Press.

Larson, Lotta C. 2010. "Digital Readers: The Next Chapter in E-Book Reading and Response." *The Reading Teacher* 64 (1): 15–22.

Meek, Margaret. 1988. *How Texts Teach What Readers Learn*. Stroud, UK: Thimble Press.

Miller, Donalyn. 2009. *The Book Whisperer: Awakening the Inner Reader in Every Child*. San Francisco: Jossey-Bass.

Myhill, Debra, Susan Jones, and Rosemary Hopper. 2006. *Talking, Listening, Learning: Effective Talk in the Primary Classroom*. Berkshire, England: Open University Press.

Newkirk, Thomas. 2012. *The Art of Slow Reading: Six Time-Honored Practices for Engagement*. Portsmouth, NH: Heinemann.

New London Group. 1996. "A Pedagogy of Multiliteracies: Designing Social Futures." *Harvard Educational Review* 66 (1): 60–92.

Nodelman, Perry. 1996. *The Pleasures of Children's Literature*. 2nd ed. White Plains, NY: London.

Nystrand, Martin. 1997. *Opening Dialogue: Understanding the Dynamics of Language and Learning in the English Classroom*. New York: Teachers College Press.

O'Reilly, Tim. 2005. "What Is Web 2.0?" Retrieved August 11, 2014 from http://oreilly.com/web2/archive/what-is-web-20.html.

Ormiston, Meg. 2011. *Creating a Digital-Rich Classroom: Teaching & Learning in a Web 2.0 World*. Bloomington, IN: Solution Tree Press.

Pennac, Daniel. 1999. *Better Than Life*. Markham, Ontario: Pembroke.

Peterson, Ralph, and Maryann Eeds. 1990. *Grand Conversations: Literature Groups in Action*. New York: Scholastic.

Piper, Andrew. 2012. *Book Was There: Reading in Electronic Times*. Chicago: University of Chicago Press.

Prensky, Marc. 2001. "Digital Natives, Digital Immigrants." *On the Horizon* 9 (5): 1–6.

Richardson, Will. 2009. *Blogs, Wikis, Podcasts, and Other Powerful Web Tools for Classrooms*. Thousand Oaks, CA: Corwin Press.

Rosen, Larry D. 2012. *iDisorder: Understanding Our Obsession with Technology and Overcoming Its Hold on Us*. New York: Palgrave MacMillan.

Santayana, George, and Martin A. Coleman, eds. 2009. *The Essential Santayana: Selected Writings*. Bloomington, IN: Indiana University Press.

Scholes, Robert. 1985. *Textual Power: Literary Theory and the Teaching of English*. New Haven: Yale University Press.

Serafini, Frank. 2001. *The Reading Workshop: Creating Space for Readers*. Portsmouth, NH: Heinemann.

———. 2004. *Lessons in Comprehension: Explicit Instruction in the Reading Workshop*. Portsmouth, NH: Heinemann.

———. 2009. *Interactive Comprehension Strategies: Fostering Meaningful Talk About Text*. New York: Scholastic.

———. 2010a. *Classroom Reading Assessments: More Efficient Ways to View and Evaluate Your Readers*. Portsmouth, NH: Heinemann.

———. 2010b. "Reading Multimodal Texts: Perceptual, Structural and Ideological Perspectives." *Children's Literature in Education* 41: 85–104.

———. 2012a. "Expanding the Four Resources Model: Reading Visual and Multimodal Texts." *Pedagogies: An International Journal* 7 (2): 150–164.

———. 2012b. "Reading Multimodal Texts in the 21st Century." *Research in the Schools* 19 (1): 26–32.

———. 2014. *Reading the Visual: An Introduction to Teaching Multimodal Literacy*. New York: Teachers College Press.

Serafini, Frank, and Cyndi Giorgis. 2003. *Reading Aloud and Beyond: Fostering the Intellectual Life with Older Readers*. Portsmouth, NH: Heinemann.

Serafini, Frank, and Suzette Youngs. 2006. *Around the Reading Workshop in 180 Days: A Month-by-Month Guide to Effective Instruction*. Portsmouth, NH: Heinemann.

Serafini, Frank, and Suzette Youngs. 2008. *More (Advanced) Lessons in Comprehension: Expanding Students' Understanding of All Types of Texts*. Portsmouth, NH: Heinemann

Smith, Frank. 1988. *Joining the Literacy Club: Further Essays into Education*. Portsmouth, NH: Heinemann.

Thompson, Terry. 2008. *Adventures in Graphica: Using Comics and Graphic Novels to Teach Comprehension, 2–6*. Portland, ME: Stenhouse.

Trelease, Jim. 1989. *The New Read-Aloud Handbook*. New York: Penguin.

Turkle, Sherry. 2011. *Alone Together: Why We Expect More from Technology and Less from Each Other*. New York: Basic Books.

Turrion, Celia. 2014. "Multimedia Book Apps in a Contemporary Culture: Commerce and Innovation, Continuity and Rupture." *Nordic Journal of ChildLit Aesthetics* 5: 1–7.

Ulin, David L. 2010. *The Lost Art of Reading: Why Books Matter in a Distracted Time*. Seattle: Sasquatch Books.

Wilde, Sandra. 2013. *Quantity and Quality: Increasing the Volume and Complexity of Students' Reading*. Portsmouth, NH: Heinemann.

Yokota, Junko, and William H. Teale. 2014. "Picture Books and the Digital World." *The Reading Teacher* 67 (8): 577–585.

CHILDREN'S LITERATURE REFERENCES

Alexie, Sherman. 2007. *The Absolutely True Diary of a Part-Time Indian*. New York: Little, Brown Books for Young Readers.

Base, Graeme. 1986. *Animalia*. New York: Abrams.

Browne, Anthony. 2001. *Voices in the Park*. New York: DK Publishing.

Carman, Patrick. 2009. *Skeleton Creek*. New York: Scholastic.

Collins, Suzanne. 2008. *The Hunger Games*. New York: Scholastic.

Gaiman, Neil. 2008. *The Graveyard Book*. New York: HarperCollins.

Kinney, Jeff. 2007. *Diary of a Wimpy Kid*. New York: Abrams.

Macaulay, David. 1990. *Black and White*. New York: Houghton Mifflin.

Sendak, Maurice. 1963. *Where the Wild Things Are*. New York: Harper & Row.